Praise

'This is truly the book that all business leaders and HR Directors should read if they are looking to understand the benefits of pay transparency for their employees and their business. Rameez is a true leader in this field in making something quite big and scary for a company, much simpler. More importantly, he will give you the confidence to make the right decisions. This book is a must-have and I am certainly looking forward to creating a culture of more trust and openness in my organisation.'

— John Athanasiou, Director of People, HarperCollins UK and Ireland

A Case of the Mondays explores a complex and emotionally charged area with a mix of humour, anecdotes and case-based insight. Fair and ethically run companies deliver long-term sustainable growth, and fair reward sits at the heart of this. Rameez shares analysis and practical advice to help leaders and HR professionals address this.'

— Nick Skinner, Senior Vice President, Human Resources, Abcam PLC

'A thought-provoking and practical guide for any HR professional embarking on a pay transparency journey in their organisation. In this book, Rameez shares his valuable insights based on years of experience, along with practical and straightforward how-to tips which will appeal to all HR professionals.'

— Lizzie Henson, Founder, HR Ninjas

'Too often, HR and business leaders are instinctively dismissive of the concept of pay transparency. In *A Case of the Mondays*, Rameez encourages leaders to challenge their thinking. Whilst being an engaging and easily readable book, he takes you through what pay transparency means, paths to achieving it and the positive impacts that getting this right will deliver. As HR professionals, it is our role to challenge long-held views, drive progress across the people agenda and, in doing so, realise commercial benefits for our businesses. This is a persuasive and practical book that I would encourage all HR and reward professionals to read.'

— Lucinda Pullinger, UK Managing Director, Instant Group

'This book presents the case well for pay transparency on the rationale for decision making. It is fundamentally important to all organisational cultures that decision making has integrity and can stand the test of scrutiny. Any feeling of discomfort regarding such transparency should be channelled into ensuring that our pay decision making has integrity and our decision making process is defendable.'

— Caren Thomas, HR Director, Chartered Insurance Institute

'This book is a must-read for all HR professionals, and many business leaders beyond. It is difficult to understand how any organisation can be serious about its DEI strategies without having a cold, hard look at pay transparency. And this is the book for that. I love how it uses a holistic approach to address the many contributing factors to what could be a complicated topic. Rameez makes it simple and easy to understand, with practical steps to align a pay transparency approach to each organisation.'

— Ed Airey, Group Employee Experience Director, National Express

'An informative and highly entertaining primer. Rameez offers clarity to the topic of pay transparency with aplomb.'

— Mustafa Jaffar, Managing Director, HR, Standard Chartered Bank

'Rameez sets out a strong argument for pay transparency and the benefits this brings in the longer term, even if in the immediate it can present as a difficult conversation. This is essential to implement a modern and progressive pay framework which is sustainable in the longer term.'

— Louise Beauchamp, Director of People, Royal College of Paediatrics and Child Health

A Case of the Mondays

How to build a culture of trust through pay transparency

Rameez Kaleem

R^ethink

First published in Great Britain in 2022 by Rethink Press
(www.rethinkpress.com)

© Copyright Rameez Kaleem

Front cover illustration courtesy of AnneMarie Walsh.

Contents

A case of the Mondays, starring:

Introduction

Can you think of a time in your current or previous role where you had a case of the Mondays? What was the reason you dreaded going into work on a Monday morning? My guess is it had something to do with lack of trust in the workplace.

My role within HR and consulting was to look at how organisations pay and reward employees. After fifteen years working in the corporate world, though, I found that my own role had stopped being rewarding.

Week after week, I was just going through the motions – not sure why I was putting together attractive pay packages for a critical candidate, only to work on a redundancy package for the same person eighteen months later, or finalising bonus calculations that included obscenely high payments for a few employees, while the organisation struggled to find room in the budget for a call centre or warehouse. At times, I was being told to approve payments that were ethically questionable.

I found my role frustrating. As HR and reward teams, my colleagues and I were not really *rewarding* our employees. We were merely reacting to the whims and gut feelings of the latest senior executive: paying bonuses or retention payments to a handful of people who were good at negotiating and handing out letters telling them they were not allowed to discuss these payments with colleagues. Meanwhile, negotiations took place with the unions on whether the remaining 99% would receive a 1% or a 1.5% pay increase.

What we were doing wasn't always fair – and it certainly wasn't transparent. Pay is an emotive topic, so naturally it makes a lot of people within organisations nervous. Pay is the deciding factor for most people when they're choosing a new role. Seeking higher pay elsewhere is often the main reason quoted by employees when they leave their jobs, but what people ultimately want to know is *that they are being treated fairly.*

What we THINK People want to know / What People REALLY want to know

How do we as HR teams demonstrate that we are treating people fairly? Transparency breeds trust. Cultivating a culture of transparency, a culture where colleagues trust each other and the leaders, can go a long way to establish our organisations as fair and inclusive.

Similarly, when it comes to pay, we build trust between colleagues by being transparent. The thought of publishing everyone's salaries and discussing them openly may scare you, but that's not what I mean. Discussing pay transparency in these binary terms devalues its wide-ranging benefits. Transparency is not the same as disclosure; transparency is about giving people context on how and why decisions are made.

What to expect from this book

In this book, we're going to talk in depth about all aspects of pay, but most importantly the concept of pay transparency. We're not just going to look at the theory, but also practical steps that you can take away to implement more pay transparency in your organisation. Pay is a topic that doesn't get talked about often, and when it does, it is usually in simplistic terms that confuse different aspects, such as equal pay and the gender pay gap (GPG).

Sceptics will argue that pay transparency is just as likely to demoralise as it is to motivate. The biggest barrier to pay transparency is reluctance and hesitation from leaders who believe most people have an inflated sense of self-worth. By comparing their salary to that of their colleagues, they will inevitably think that their pay is well below where it should be. Even publishing a broad pay range makes these leaders nervous. Pay transparency will lead employees to be demotivated and less productive, they say. In this book, we will dispel this and other myths.

Pay transparency is a journey that is different for each organisation depending on where we're starting from and our organisational culture. It is a gradual process that needs careful consideration and clear communication to employees. We cannot suddenly move from a culture of secrecy to complete transparency.

Even something as beneficial as a healthy diet can lead to adverse side effects such as fatigue and dizziness if we make a sudden change. This is because the sudden change is not sustainable and we soon resort to old habits such as binge-eating. We need to plan our diet carefully and make incremental changes. Similarly, pay transparency requires careful planning and gradual change.

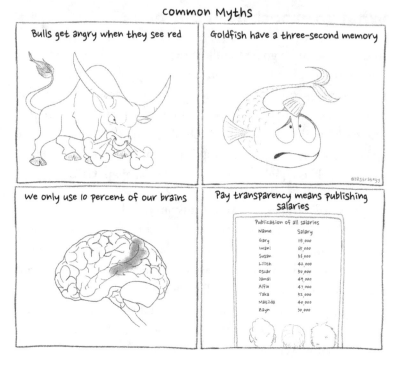

As we've touched on before, the fact is, most people are not that concerned with what everyone else is getting paid. What they want to know is that they're being treated fairly. We demonstrate fairness by being transparent about how and why pay decisions are made.

Let's assume that the concerns some leaders have about employees being paid below the market rate are true. US survey data from Payscale found that employees who were paid less than the market rate had a job satisfaction score of 40%, but when leaders actually sat down with these employees and talked to them, explaining the reasons for lower pay, their job satisfaction rose to 82%.[1] Even when people are paid less than the market rate, they are much

---

1   Holub, A, 'Why pay transparency is a good thing', *Payscale*, (23 November 2015) www.payscale.com/career-advice/why-pay-transparency-is-a-good-thing, accessed 4 April 2022

What People THINK Pay Transparency Is

What Pay Transparency REALLY Is

more satisfied when their leaders are open and transparent about pay – and it doesn't cost a penny. Pay transparency can transform organisational culture, leading to more collaboration, diversity and productivity in the workplace.

In 2015, I finally quit my job and set up my own pay and reward consultancy, 3R Strategy, in pursuit of this goal. At 3R Strategy our vision is to transform company culture through pay transparency, building a world where leaders take a fair and equitable approach to pay, and communicate clearly and honestly with their employees.

In Part One of this book, we'll discuss why HR is so crucial and why it should carry the torch for pay transparency. However, we cannot look at pay in isolation. Pay is often used to drive certain behaviours or achieve common objectives, but without clarity, pay alone won't solve all our problems. We must also look at organisational purpose and culture.

In Part Two, we'll take a deep dive into the concept of pay transparency: why we need it, the benefits and what we can learn about it from football (soccer if you're in the United States). We will also examine different elements of pay and why they're important. We will discuss the levels of pay transparency that organisations can offer. There is no wrong or right answer, but in today's world, where a lot of pay data is freely available, a total lack of transparency around pay is no longer an option.

In Part Three, you'll find practical tools and a roadmap to help you introduce pay transparency in your organisation. This part will cover the policies and processes you'll need to become more transparent, as well as step-by-step instructions that HR teams can use to build a culture of trust, collaboration and productivity.

To clarify, I'm not advocating that leaders publish the salaries of all their employees. For many people and in many cultures, salary information is personal. Disclosing it should be a personal choice.

Some employees are going to talk about pay. Do we want them to speculate, gossip and make assumptions about our intentions or do we want to be transparent and shape that conversation instead of reacting to it every time?

There are no secrets to building trust

Films are a great form of entertainment and escapism, but we underestimate the influence these stories and characters have on us. It is a concept known as narrative transportation. The idea that we become so involved in a storyline that even after we have finished watching the film or reading the story, it influences our behaviours and attitudes.

From a young age, films have always had a strong influence on me. I have also been fascinated by the portrayal and stereotypes of various characters in films. I vividly remember specific scenes and dialogues from various films. Some of these references are used throughout this book. Yes, I'm not ashamed to say that incorporating my love of films in this book is an attempt to make the topic of pay more entertaining.

Christopher Nolan's *The Prestige* is a film about two rival magicians, Robert Angier and Alfred Borden.[2] Robert is a mediocre magician but a great showman, while Alfred is a great magician but has no stage presence. The film follows the career and relationship of these two men who ultimately don't trust each other.

Alfred develops a new trick called the Transported Man in which he walks through a door on one side of the stage and instantly emerges from a door on the other side. Robert is desperate to find out how Alfred performs this trick. He gets his assistant Olivia to spy on Alfred and find out the secret behind the Transported Man. When Olivia asks why Alfred would trust her, Robert replies, 'Because you're going to tell him the truth.'

It's that simple. To build trust, all you need to do is to tell the truth.

---

2   Nolan, C, *The Prestige* (2006)

PART ONE
FINDING FULFILMENT AT WORK

1

A Culture Based On Trust

3 December 2012

At 6.30am, my radio alarm goes off and *Give Me Love* by Ed Sheeran is playing. Fifteen minutes later, my phone alarm sounds and I hit snooze.

This is my daily ritual. A radio alarm followed by a phone alarm. Dragging myself out of bed in the morning is a struggle – particularly on a Monday – but today is my first day in a new job, so a third alarm is set to go off at 7am. I can't be late today.

I finally get up, shave and put on my brand-new suit and tie. Work starts at 9am, but I allow myself a buffer and leave the house at 7.45am. I shouldn't be worried. It's not like I'm a graduate; I'm joining the head office of a global organisation in a fairly senior role. I've met the entire team already, but who doesn't want to make a good impression on their first day?

The train is packed, but I reach my station by 8.30am and I'm relieved. I have time to grab an egg sandwich on my way to the office and get to my desk at 8.45am. A new job, new colleagues, new beginning. I sit down with a smile on my face, looking across at my manager. He seems annoyed.

'You're late,' he says.

'Late?' I reply.

'Yes,' he says. 'The directors arrive at 8.30am. If the directors come in and see we're not here, it doesn't look good.'

'I'm sorry,' I say. 'The contract said 9am, so I thought I was early.'

'No, the start time is 8.30am.'

Part of me wants to let this go, but the other part tells me not to start my first day with a misunderstanding. To make sure I'm not late again, I email the HR team to confirm my start time and they reply saying it is 9am. In an attempt to defuse the situation and avoid future misunderstandings, I then speak to my manager.

'I checked and my start time is 9am, but if you would like me to come in at 8.30am, then of course I'm happy to do that. Shall I come in at 8.30am from tomorrow?'

My manager's face goes blank. I'm generally good at reading people and guessing from their expression what might come next, but on this occasion I'm clueless. I'm waiting for a response. Before I know it, my manager is on the phone to HR, arguing that I'm late to work. Is this really happening on my first day in the job?

Putting things in perspective: Five months previously, I was living in Snagovo, a small village in Bosnia and Herzegovina. I was on an international volunteer programme to learn about how the people in Bosnia were still rebuilding their lives after the war and genocide in Srebrenica, where 8,372 Muslims were killed by the Serb army.[3]

I would wake up in the morning and have breakfast with my Bosnian family. This comprised warm bread, cheese and strong

---

3   'What happened in Srebrenica', Remembering Srebrenica,
https:/srebrenica.org.uk/what-happened/history/happened-srebrenica, accessed 30 June 2022

coffee. The traditional way to drink Bosnian coffee is to put a sugar cube in your mouth, and then sip the drink so the sugar dissolves to dilute the strong taste. I then worked on the farm all day, often in temperatures over 35°C, cutting and collecting grass to make haystacks.

We were building a strawberry farm, which we had raised funds for in the UK. It sounds a lot more glamorous than it was: the actual building of the strawberry farm involved days of shovelling manure across the field. Once the soil was ready, we spent hours on our knees planting the strawberries. In between, there were other tasks to carry out, such as herding sheep. I even milked a cow!

Towards the end of my stay, I visited the cemetery in Srebrenica: a never-ending sea of identical white marble gravestones where the victims of the genocide were buried. I had met with many survivors of the genocide and victims of sexual violence who had lost their entire families in the conflict. Families who had been buried in mass graves and later, in an attempt to hide the war crimes, dug up and transported to secondary mass graves. As a result, most survivors were unable to bury their loved ones' bodies with dignity – in many cases finding only one body part, identified through DNA testing.

Despite the horror they had lived through, these people showed incredible resolve, hope and optimism for a better future. Here I was a few months later, stressed and annoyed over something so trivial: my start time at work and the prospect of a manager who I clearly wasn't going to get along with. I find it difficult to work in an environment where there is a lack of trust. In this case, it was not something I was willing to put up with. I resigned.

My situation wasn't unique. Millions of us find ourselves stuck in jobs with a toxic culture and poor leadership, many just accepting it. 'It's only a job,' we say. 'I'll stay for two years so it doesn't look bad on my CV, and then look for something else. I'm still early in my career and this is what we must all put up with. Eventually, life will be much easier in the corporate world.' These are just some of the arguments we use to rationalise our situation. To persevere. Where is our hope and optimism?

Why is it so difficult to find organisations with a culture based on trust? A culture of trust means giving our colleagues the autonomy to do their jobs. It means trusting ourselves as HR professionals and our recruitment teams to hire the right people.

Global analytics firm Gallup defines engaged employees as 'those who are involved in, enthusiastic about and committed to their work and workplace'.[4] Based on over fifty years of employee engagement research, Gallup knows that engaged employees produce significantly better business outcomes, but only 15% of employees worldwide fall in the 'engaged' category.

That's a depressingly low percentage. It's no surprise, then, that the film *Office Space* – centred around a group of disgruntled employees doing monotonous work and being managed by multiple bosses – became a cult hit.[5] Initech, where they all work, is a company with poor management, bad communication and low employee morale. The protagonist, Peter Gibbons, describes how work feels like a prison sentence, admitting to his therapist that 'every day is the worst day of my life'.

In a meeting with consultants Bob and Bob, Peter tells them that when he makes a mistake, he has eight different people telling him about it and his only real motivation at work is not to be hassled.

---

4   Royal, K, 'Who's responsible for employee engagement', *Gallup* (14 September 2019), www.gallup.com/workplace/266822/engaged-employees-differently.aspx, accessed 4 April 2022

5   Judge, M, *Office Space* (20th Century Studios, 1999)

That makes him work just hard enough not to get fired. How many of our employees feel and act the same way?

One of the reasons *Office Space* is so beloved is because it's something many people can relate to. Who hasn't come across an arrogant or obnoxious leader? Who hasn't felt lost at their work desk or cubicle, producing endless reports without a real sense of purpose? Who hasn't become emotionally attached to a stapler or felt the urge to take a baseball bat to a printer after yet another paper jam? Who hasn't had a case of the Mondays?

A case of the Mondays

Building trust in the workplace

The example of my own case of the Mondays was due to poor leadership in a toxic and secretive organisational culture. A culture where there was no trust.

There are many reasons why people around the world dread Sunday evenings when they realise they have to go into work the following day. Can you remember a time in your current or previous job when you had a case of the Mondays? Was it due to a poor relationship with your manager, team members or office politics? Whatever the reason, it probably had something to do with a lack of trust. To find fulfilment in the workplace and avoid having a case of the Mondays, we need relationships built on trust.

How do we build trust in the workplace? Where do we start? Why not start with possibly the most important aspect of a job and often the first thing that people see when they are applying for a new role – what they will get paid? This doesn't mean an environment where people know what everyone else gets paid. Transparency means giving people context. If we can't be fair and transparent with this, then we're already off to a bad start in our working relationship with colleagues.

When we're transparent, we show our colleagues that we have nothing to hide because our process is fair and equitable. One thing to keep in mind, though: if trust has already broken down, then no amount of pay transparency is going to fix it on its own.

A business case for HR

Life is too short to work in a job we hate. Employees can't do what Peter Gibbons does in *Office Space* and sleep all day instead of going to work or knock down the walls of their cubicles to get more daylight. If they did, they would probably be sent to see you or one of your colleagues in HR.

As HR professionals, we're partially responsible for everyone who works at the company, so whether people are happy or miserable in their jobs is to some extent down to us. It's scary to think of it that way, but as Spider-Man always says, 'With great power comes great responsibility'.[6]

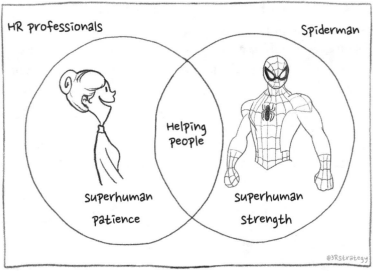

How can we, as HR professionals, do something about employee engagement when we're stuck in a policing role, managing grievances, dismissals, redundancies and consultations? Meanwhile, the reward team is saddled with coordinating pay reviews, bonuses and the sensitive matter of executive compensation.

A career in HR is not easy. Employee conflicts, unreasonable demands from line managers and inappropriate behaviours abound. Let's face it, most people are difficult when they have a problem and they're unhappy – and they generally only contact HR when there's a problem and they're unhappy. Has anyone ever

---

6   Straczynski, JM, *The Amazing Spider-Man* (vol 2, #38) (Marvel, 2002)

booked a meeting with you to thank you for their monthly payslip arriving on time? I doubt it, but if it's a day late, you'll hear all about it.

Why did you go into HR? Did you fall into it or make a conscious decision? If it was a conscious decision, I'm guessing it's because like most HR professionals, you realise the old cliché that 'an organisation is only as good as its people' is true. However, instead of working to improve the culture of your organisation and develop your people, you've probably ended up becoming the traffic warden of the corporate world.

In the film *Lock, Stock and Two Smoking Barrels*,[7] there is a scene where a traffic warden attempts to give a ticket to the driver of a getaway van, asking him to move. The getaway driver realises that persuasion is futile, smacks the traffic warden on the head and puts

---

7   Ritchie, G, *Lock, Stock and Two Smoking Barrels* (PolyGram, 1998)

him in the back of the van. Later, the gang realises that along with all the cash, there is a traffic warden in the van and asks what he is doing there. They can't decide what to do until one person says, 'I hate traffic wardens', and all three of them jump in the back of the van and beat him up.

The moral of the story? Nobody tends to like a pedantic traffic warden. We need to focus on the big picture and avoid becoming traffic wardens of the corporate world: drones who won't empathise or listen to reason, but simply enforce policies for our 'resources'.

Retention is cheaper than recruitment

How do we find time to focus on the big picture and the reason we love our profession? How do we reward, recognise and retain our people? How do we create a working environment where instead of facing the same frustrations every day, employees (HR included) wake up inspired to go to work, and feel rewarded and appreciated and supported by leaders who take the time to develop and empower them when they get there?

In many organisations, HR is neglected. There's often one HR person responsible for managing hundreds of employees, and as a result, employee engagement scores plummet. Employee turnover continues to rise and recruitment costs escalate.

Research from *Oxford Economics* found that the average cost of replacing a single employee is over £30,000.[8] This includes loss of productivity, advertising, agency fees, HR and management time. The cost goes up as we look at more technical and senior roles that take longer to recruit.

8   'The cost of brain drain', *Oxford Economics* (3 March 2014), www.oxfordeconomics.com/recent-releases/the-cost-of-brain-drain, accessed 4 April 2022

The PERCEIVED cost of Recruitment

The REAL cost of Recruitment

Recruitment fee

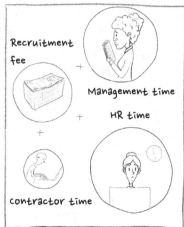

Recruitment fee

+

Management time

+

HR time

+

contractor time

Even if you feel that this estimate is on the high side, there is no doubt that retaining your key employees is more cost-effective than replacing them on a regular basis. If hiring an extra HR person enables you to retain only two more people a year, they will have covered their cost, but the truth is that having a larger HR team with the capacity to focus on employees adds so much more value to the business. Not just to the people who may be thinking of leaving, but all your colleagues.

That's not to say that employee turnover should be zero. There will always be some people who leave your organisation for one reason or another, and having new people come in with fresh ideas and perspectives is healthy, but a lot of employee turnover, particularly from exceptional colleagues, can be avoided.

There is a wealth of research on the positive correlation between employee engagement and organisational turnover and growth.[9]

9   Harter, J and Mann, A, 'The Right Culture: Not Just About Employee Satisfaction', Gallup Workplace (12 April 2017), www.gallup.com/workplace/236366/right-culture-not-employee-satisfaction.aspx, accessed 30 June 2022

Leaders of successful organisations realise this and proactively invest in HR to look after and engage their people. The alternative is a working environment where people feel disengaged, disillusioned and demotivated. A place like Initech where every day is progressively worse than the day before.

Investing in an HR function that has a strategic role as well as an operational one is a no-brainer. Entrepreneur and chief executive officer (CEO) of VaynerMedia, Gary Vaynerchuk, talks about the fact that in most organisations, the number-two role to the CEO is the chief financial officer, but in his organisation, it is an HR role: the chief heart officer.[10]

If you work in an organisation where the CEO, like Gary Vaynerchuk, is already people-focused and sees HR as a vital function, then you're in luck. But what if your CEO is more like Michael Scott of Dunder Mifflin Paper Company, the fictional organisation from *The Office: An American Workplace*?[11] Michael Scott *hates* the branch HR representative, Toby Flendersen. In one interview, Michael explains that because Toby works in HR, he technically works for corporate and therefore isn't part of the Dunder Mifflin Scranton family.

Plus, he adds, 'Also, he's divorced, so he's really not a part of *his* family.'

Michael just wants a positive work environment where every day is fun and exciting, and everyone likes him. He thinks HR – in this case, Toby – sucks the fun out of work and 'makes the office lame'. In other words, he sees Toby as a traffic warden.

10   Bolger, B, 'Gary Vaynerchuk: Winner of the ISO 10018 Honorary CEO Citation for Quality People Management', *ESM*, www.enterpriseengagement.org/Gary-Vaynerchuk-Winner-of-the-ISO-10018-Honorary-CEO-Citation-for-Quality-People-Management/, accessed 30 June 2022

11   Daniels, G, *The Office: An American Workplace* Season 02 Episode 02 (NBC Universal, 2005)

Convincing this type of CEO that HR adds real value to the organisation is going to be a challenge. It starts by demonstrating that we're not stereotypical 'traffic wardens', but can help create an environment where people love to work, wake up every day inspired, and offer their blood, sweat and tears because they buy into our mission.

This is no easy task. There's a lot to do to achieve it, and although we can take the lead, HR teams can't do it alone. We need the rest of the organisation to come with us on the journey. As HR teams, we have so much on our plate already: recruitment, employment law, training and development, diversity and inclusion. In this book, we are going to focus on one essential element: pay transparency as a means of transforming our organisational culture.

Some organisations have tried to rebrand HR, renaming roles to alternatives such as people manager, head of people operations or, like VaynerMedia, chief heart officer, but we need more than just a new name. The theme of this book, transparency, is aimed at building a more human-centric approach. Many successful organisations, such as Netflix and Google, have discovered that this human-centric approach makes good business sense.

We often hear that HR, the people function, should be learning more about the business and commercial side of the organisation and using data and technology. This is true, but it's also time for the organisation as a whole to start learning more about people.

Before we can bring about meaningful change in our organisations, we need a clear understanding of what needs to happen, why and how. We will cover all of this in the next two sections of this book. In Part Three we will go through the steps we use at 3R Strategy to introduce pay transparency and build a culture of trust. You can use this concise breakdown of 3R Strategy's approach and strategies for whatever you hope to implement in your organisation.

Most importantly, we need to understand how essential and inspiring the world of HR can be. Making work meaningful and productive for employees, and in doing so, contributing to our success, we have the power to shift the direction of our organisations entirely.

2

A Sense Of Purpose

John F Kennedy was visiting National Aeronautics and Space Administration (NASA) in 1961 when he came across an employee in the hallway wearing a NASA badge. When JFK casually asked him what he did at NASA, the employee replied 'I'm helping put a man on the moon, Mr President.'[12]

JFK then noticed that the employee was carrying a broom and asked him about his job. The employee explained that he was the janitor. Imagine a company where the cleaner feels just as connected to its purpose as the CEO.

We all play a different role within an organisation, but people fundamentally want to know that what they are doing serves a greater purpose. As Simon Sinek says in his book *Start With Why*, people don't love their jobs because of *what* they do. They love their jobs because of *why* they do it and how they *feel* when they are at work, either physically or virtually.[13]

At NASA, every employee – janitor included – knows they are contributing to a greater purpose and they are in this together,

12   Gallo, C, '18,000 Pages of NASA Archives Uncover JFK's Speech Strategy That Inspired The Moon Landing, *Forbes*, www.forbes.com/sites/carminegallo/2018/10/11/18000-pages-of-nasa-archives-uncovers-jfks-speech-strategy-that-inspired-the-moon-landing, accessed 30 June 2022

13   Sinek, S, *Start With Why: How great leaders inspire everyone to take action* (Portfolio, 2009)

because NASA treats its employees like adults by being honest and transparent with them. In 2020, NASA was named the best place to work in the US federal government for the ninth consecutive year.[14]

Why purpose?

You may be wondering why there is a chapter on purpose in a book about pay transparency. There are two main reasons for this.

Pay is critical for all employees. It pays the bills. It is the determining factor for most people when they accept a job offer, but once they're settled, the paycheque is less motivating. They will only stay in a job for so long if they're bored and miserable, so as HR professionals, we cannot just look at pay in isolation. A clear sense of purpose, both individually and at an organisational level, is critical.

Secondly, we often hear purpose and pay pitched as opposites. For example, we can find a job that gives us a real sense of purpose, perhaps in the charity sector, but we may have to sacrifice on pay. Alternatively, we can compromise and accept a role that we may not identify with or we find boring, but take home a great salary. However, this trend is changing. Organisations are realising that pay and purpose must go hand in hand and fewer people are now willing to compromise.

What is your organisation's vision? A good vision statement can inspire loyalty and innovation, provide a sense of purpose, and help to define short- and long-term goals, but many organisations have vision statements that are unnecessarily long and meaningless. They

---

14   'NASA Named Best Place to Work, No 1 for COVID-19 Response', NASA, www.nasa.gov/press-release/nasa-named-best-place-to-work-no-1-for-covid-19-response, accessed 30 June 2022

just explain what the organisation does. A good vision statement articulates what your organisation and people are working towards that will make the world a better place.

A vision is aspirational. We may never achieve it in our lifetime, but it sets the destination. At 3R Strategy, our vision is a world where organisations build a culture of trust through pay transparency.

Finding a sense of purpose

A few years into my working career, I started to feel disillusioned. I was doing well and had good colleagues, but there was nothing inspiring or fulfilling about my work. There was no real sense of purpose.

After a few years, I decided to look for a sense of purpose elsewhere. I explored various options and eventually found myself volunteering at a supplementary Saturday school, teaching Year 9 English to children from disadvantaged backgrounds. I'm an introvert and standing in front of a group of curious and often naughty teenagers was quite intimidating, but I had a purpose. This was not only to address educational disadvantage, but to act as a role model and mentor to these children who would be able to make a positive impact in their communities. I decided to stick with it and began reading teaching books, watching YouTube training videos and developing more structured lesson plans.

Gradually, I got more comfortable in the classroom. After a couple of years, it became the highlight of my week. I would wake up every Saturday and look forward to going to class.

Do you have a sense of purpose at work? If not, what do you do outside of work that gives you a sense of purpose?

I can't tell you what to do outside of work, but I can advise you on what not to do. In one organisation, a leader needed to access a team member's inbox to find a password. Upon accessing their inbox, she discovered they had been using their work email address to run a satanic cult. I can't say whether the team member found inspiration in that activity – but in the process, they lost their job.

Volunteering is a great way to develop skills and find a sense of purpose, but why can't we get this from our jobs? Is it so impossible that we could all find work where we feel part of a cause or vision we believe in? Where we do things to help others, be they colleagues, clients or partners?

Why is volunteering such an effective way to find a sense of purpose and fulfilment? Because purpose and fulfilment come from believing in the greater meaning of an action and helping others in the process. They come from a culture of collaboration and trust where people support each other to achieve collective success. This sense of purpose is so powerful that millions of people around the world give up hours of their time every week – even when they're not getting paid.

Having a sense of purpose in the workplace comes from working in an organisation with a vision you identify with. Then it doesn't matter whether you're a technical engineer or a receptionist, a CEO or a caretaker.

I volunteered as a teacher at the supplementary school for eight years, at which point I took on the role of head. Now I was working Monday to Friday in my day job and spending my whole weekend either managing the school or preparing for the following week. The school had over 100 students from Year 4 to A-level, more than twenty-five volunteers and several parents to speak to every week.

Yes, up to thirty volunteers came to teach at the school every Saturday. In some cases, they were commuting for over an hour, paying their own travel and parking expenses to do a job they were not getting paid for. At one point, I had a waiting list of ten volunteers who wanted to teach at the school. I had to tell them that we just had no space available.

Meanwhile, in my day job, I was constantly tasked with putting together attractive pay and retention packages as the organisation was struggling to recruit people and retain existing employees.

I'm not saying that if we instil a sense of purpose and have inspiring vision statements, people will flock to our organisations and be prepared to work for no money. We all need an income to survive and pay the bills. We need holidays to recharge, but we also need to grow and be challenged. That's why pay and purpose must go hand in hand, purpose being the starting point. In my experience of volunteering, and the experience of many others, there is a compelling case demonstrating the power of purpose, the importance of which is only going to get stronger.[15]

Purpose is just as powerful as pay

A study from the Society for Human Resource Management tells us that 94% of Millennials want to use their skills to benefit a cause.[16] They want to know that their work is making a difference and improving the lives of other people. They believe the primary purpose of businesses should be improving society over generating profit.

15 'Volunteering and Mental Wellness', Project Helping, https://projecthelping.org/benefits-of-volunteering, accessed 29 June 2022

16 Gurchiek, K, 'Millennial's desire to do good defines workplace culture', *SHRM* (7 July 2014), www.shrm.org/resourcesandtools/hr-topics/behavioral-competencies/global-and-cultural-effectiveness/pages/millennial-impact.aspx, accessed 4 April 2022

A study by WeSpire, an employee-experience platform, found that Generation Z – the generation succeeding Millennials – has an even stronger attachment to purpose.[17] In fact, this is the first generation to prioritise purpose over salary. They need to see a connection between their work and its social impact, and a positive work culture is twice as important to them as a higher salary when it comes to retention. When people don't find a sense of purpose at work, they go in search of it elsewhere. Some find it through volunteering opportunities; others find another job. All this points to one thing: organisations need to cultivate a strong sense of purpose and a commitment to social responsibility or people will eventually leave and look for it in another organisation.

As well as delivering a strong sense of purpose, supporting your community through donations and giving employees time off for volunteering will go a long way towards building a positive workplace. In Part Two, we will discuss how having an approach that starts with purpose will form a critical part of pay and reward strategies in the future.

Culture and values

Jerry Maguire is a rich and successful sports agent who appears to have everything.[18] He's never been so happy to be alive, but something is not quite right. He's becoming disillusioned with a cynical world where sports stars are more interested in endorsements than giving an autograph to children.

One long night in a hotel room, he writes a mission statement

---

17   '15 insights into Gen Z, purpose, and the future of work', *WeSpire*,
www.wespire.com/15-insights-gen-z-purpose-and-future-of-work, accessed 30 June 2022

18   Crowe, C, *Jerry Maguire* (1996)

demanding a more human approach to business. Jerry Maguire doesn't hate his job. On the contrary, he loves it. He just feels that they need to rethink their culture and values – an adjustment of mind and attitude.

We flashback to Jerry's mentor, the late great Dicky Fox, who says, 'If this is empty' pointing to his heart, 'this doesn't matter' tapping his head. Jerry Maguire has a sense of purpose, but he's disillusioned by *how* the company and his colleagues go about doing their jobs.

The 'how' is defined by your values – the principles you will abide by no matter what. They are your deep-held beliefs that drive your behaviours and decision making. The collective behaviours of all your employees become your organisation's culture.

Culture must align with pay

Just like purpose, culture must align with pay. When introducing a culture change or reinforcing an existing culture, leaders can use pay to encourage certain behaviours from colleagues.

There's no point having values on wall plaques or in handbooks if they are not actioned. For example, Enron's values were 'Communication. Respect. Integrity. Excellence.'[19] Enron was ranked the fifth largest organisation in the US in 2002, but collapsed after a massive accounting fraud scheme was uncovered. There was evidence of how executives pocketed millions of dollars from off-the-books partnerships while reporting inflated profits to shareholders. There was no evidence of integrity.

---

19   Kunen, J, 'Enron's Vision (and Values) Thing, *The New York Times* (19 January 2002), www.nytimes.com/2002/01/19/opinion/enron-s-vision-and-values-thing.html, accessed 30 June 2022

Your organisation's values form its brand identity and must be lived by each employee. These values must be easy to understand and made explicit through leadership behaviours. Now more than ever, with so many people working remotely, you need your colleagues to connect with your organisation's values as you work towards a shared vision.

What We THINK Having Values Means   What it Actually Means

How clear are your values?

A few years ago, I was running a workshop with the management team of a relatively small organisation. We talked about organisational values and the management team was comfortable that they had a clear set of values, even though they were not written down.

I then ran a survey with approximately forty employees; almost everyone had a different view on the company's values. There was also a stark contrast between the views of the management team and the employees who, for the first time, were able to provide completely honest feedback in an anonymised survey. This example shows that while leadership teams may think they have a clear set of values, they are often either not as clear as they think or not communicated effectively across the organisation.

Earlier in this chapter, we talked about how a sense of purpose is important for Millennials and appears to be even stronger in Generation Z. The same WeSpire survey found that Generation Z employees expect consistency and transparency and will call you out, sometimes publicly, if they feel the company is hiding something.

When we look at our organisations' approach to pay in the next part of this book, we will consider how some elements of pay and reward can be used to drive certain behaviours. Before we do this, though, we need to have a clear purpose, set of values and a culture we aspire to, so we know what behaviours we want to drive through our reward strategy.

Now that we've established the importance of starting with a strong sense of purpose and being clear about our culture, let's dive into the focus of this book: how we manage pay and create a culture of trust through pay transparency.

PART TWO
PAY, PERFORMANCE AND PROGRESSION

3

Pay Transparency

Set in Alabama in the 1930s, *To Kill a Mockingbird* is the story of Atticus Finch, a white lawyer defending a black man, Tom Robinson, accused of raping a white woman.[20] The story is narrated by Atticus's daughter, Scout. We see the good and evil of the world through the eyes of a six-year-old child and her ten-year-old brother, Jem.

Early on, we learn that Atticus is a virtuous man. From his actions both at home and in the courtroom, it is clear that Atticus is an authentic and honest individual. Through his truthfulness, he is held up as the ethical standard that every character should seek to embody. Even his parenting style is unique as he treats his children as adults, answering all of their questions honestly. He trusts them with the truth and seeks opportunities for them to exercise their judgement.

Atticus tells his brother, 'Children are children, but they can spot an evasion quicker than adults.' Atticus Finch, a true American hero, believes in transparency.

---

20   Lee, H, *To Kill a Mockingbird* (JB Lippincott & Co, 1960)

Why do we need pay transparency?

Pay transparency means being clear and open about how and why we make pay decisions. What makes a lot of leaders nervous about pay transparency is the worry that people will find out what everyone earns, but the fact is, most people are not that concerned with what everyone else is getting paid. What they are concerned with is whether they're being treated fairly – and we as HR professionals demonstrate fairness by being transparent about how and why we make pay decisions.

From an employee perspective, pay transparency leads to fairness because when we're open and transparent, we show that we have nothing to hide. The pay process is fair and equitable. With pay transparency, we're not just sharing the outcomes, but also our thought process, and that builds trust with employees.

Employees have instant access to a wealth of salary data from websites like Glassdoor and Indeed. While some organisations continue to ask people to keep their pay information confidential, many employees openly discuss pay and reward with their colleagues. Leaders need the tools to deliver the right messages to their people, so they can shape some of that conversation instead of reacting to it every time.

A Payscale survey found one of the top predictors of employee engagement is an organisation's ability to communicate clearly and honestly about pay.[21] Even when employees were paid below the market rate, if someone took the time to talk to them about pay and explain why, the survey showed job satisfaction numbers more than doubled – rising from 40% to 82%.

---

21   'The surprising truth about employee engagement', Payscale, www.payscale.com/research-and-insights/infographic-employee-engagement, accessed May 2022

Yes, even when people are being paid less than the market rate, they are more satisfied when their organisation is transparent about pay. What does this tell us?

Having a fair, pay and reward framework is only part of the solution. It also needs to be communicated clearly. In the absence of a clear communication strategy, how do people know that the process is fair? They may form their own perceptions.

Context about how and why pay decisions are made enables people to do their jobs more effectively. More pay transparency equals more job satisfaction – and lower employee turnover as a result.

Do we need to publish salaries?

If people are more concerned with *how* and *why* decisions are made, do we need to publish the salaries of all employees? Pay is not a simple one-dimensional process. There are many variables that could determine pay, such as:

- Skills and capabilities

- Task complexity

- Performance

- External market

- Our organisation's position against the market (eg median, upper quartile)

- Internal equity

- Affordability

Measuring these factors in organisations is difficult and often subjective. For example, how do we measure performance? If performance influences pay, how can we ensure that leaders are managing performance fairly and consistently?

If we want to look at the external market, what data should we use? Industry-specific or all industries? Is that the same for all roles or are some roles different from others? If we publish salaries or pay ranges, should we offer training to everyone in our organisation around how salary surveys are compiled and how to benchmark?

Then there is the question of privacy. How many of us tell our friends and family how much we get paid? Would we want to tell our colleagues? Research from the Fawcett Society found that around 50% of people felt uncomfortable disclosing their salary to a peer,[22] in which case, shouldn't disclosing our salaries be a personal decision, rather than one made unilaterally by the organisation?

Being transparent about pay doesn't mean we have to tell people what everyone else gets paid – particularly if it's going to make many people uncomfortable.

That said, we do need to be clear about how and why pay decisions are made. People want to know that there is a sound process – fairness and consistency. They want to know that their livelihoods are not subject to bias or the 'gut feeling' of their line manager, which begs the question: how do we ensure fairness and consistency?

What football can teach us about pay transparency

There's a lot we can learn from professional football when it comes to pay. Footballers expect to have their salaries published online – and by the press – for their teammates and everyone else to see. Argentine footballer Lionel Messi gets paid over £500,000 a week – considerably more than his teammates. How can such a high salary be justified? What about equal pay?

Professional football has clear performance indicators. The skill of each player is there for all of us to see. As teams do well, they get promoted to higher leagues that require greater skill, resulting in higher salaries, but even within the same league – and within the same team – there is an abundance of data available on

22 'Fawcett launches equal pay advice service as research reveals 1 in 3 workers are unaware pay discrimination is illegal', Fawcett Society (9 November 2018), www.fawcettsociety.org.uk/news/fawcett-launches-equal-pay-advice-service-as-research-reveals-1-in-3-workers-are-unaware-of-rights, accessed May 2022

performance: goals, assists, passes, completion rates, tackles and so on.

How Do We Measure Performance?

The Ivory Coast footballer Didier Drogba, who was named African Footballer of the Year in 2006 and 2009, talked about how before every match, his manager used to put up the names of the top three scorers of the opposition team.[23] On one occasion, before the team played Barcelona, the names went up as usual – Xavi on fourteen, Sánchez and Fàbregas on fifteen.

'We all laughed when the top scorer came up – Lionel Messi on sixty-three goals,' he said.

Messi's teammates, as well as everyone else, could clearly see the contribution he made, and his teammates all reaped the benefits.

23   Sidle, R, 'Didier Drogba's Story About Preparing For Lionel Messi Is Incredible', *Sport Bible* (20 February 2018), www.sportbible.com/football/news-legends-didier-drogbas-story-about-preparing-for-lionel-messi-is-incredible-20180220, accessed 30 June 2022

With Messi's contribution, Barcelona won numerous cups and titles. If Messi hadn't been paid a higher salary than his teammates, he might have left and joined another club, jeopardising the future success of the other Barcelona players.

The office environment is – pardon the pun – a completely different ballgame. We don't have cameras at our desks with commentators and statisticians observing our every move. We may sit opposite colleagues for years and never really know the contribution they are making or their level of performance.

We tend to form perceptions based on limited work-related interactions or, worse, on things completely unrelated to work. We could be sitting next to the Messi of finance or the Messi of marketing, but all we know is that they make a terrible cup of tea. That could lead us to believe they must be bad at their job as well. If they can't even make a decent cup of tea, how can they manage a team?

A study published in *Harvard Business Review* asked 700 Silicon Valley engineers to rate their performance relative to their peers.[24] An astonishing 92% thought they were in the upper quartile (top 25%), while 40% thought they were in the top 5%. *That's 280 people who thought they ranked in the top thirty-five.*

This shows us that in the absence of clear and transparent performance/skill indicators, publishing salaries could cause chaos, with people feeling they are undervalued compared to colleagues who they perceive to be adding less value to the organisation.

---

24   Zenger, T, 'The case against pay transparency', *Harvard Business Review* (30 September 2016), https:/hbr.org/2016/09/the-case-against-pay-transparency, accessed May 2022

Publishing Salaries WITHOUT context

Publishing Salaries WITH context

So, what does professional football teach us about how we manage pay in the workplace? It teaches us that if we want more pay transparency or even complete transparency, we need clear and obvious indicators about performance. A once-yearly meeting, where employees receive an arbitrary rating along a forced distribution curve without knowing how or why that decision was made, just doesn't cut it. As an HR professional, how many times have you been in a meeting or a calibration session where two managers have a completely different view on the performance of the same employee?

We need clear indicators of the skills and competencies people need to carry out their roles successfully in different parts of the organisation. Do we need people to be better at collaborating, managing diverse relationships or problem solving? How will they develop those skills and competencies as they progress in the organisation? How will they be measured objectively, so we don't just promote people based on who the manager thinks is the best 'fit' for the team without any guidance or data?

Our challenge as HR professionals is convincing senior leaders that pay transparency is good for our people and good for the entire organisation. We have to address their biggest fear, showing them that pay transparency *doesn't* mean sharing what everyone gets paid, but being clear about how and why we make pay decisions.

Sometimes, when leaders carry out salary benchmarking exercises, they find that many of their people are earning below their chosen market position and do not want to say anything to employees. It's only natural to worry in this scenario. After all, HR and the senior management team have all the information in front of them – and it doesn't look great. What will employees think when they realise they are not even at the mid-point of the pay range?

This brings us back to the Payscale survey, which found that organisations paying below-market salaries but clearly communicating why this was the case still had 82% satisfied employees compared to 40% in the absence of clear communication. Isn't that incredible? So many people feel satisfied despite knowing that their salary is below the market rate. This just goes to show the impact we can have on our people by treating them like adults, being open and transparent, and explaining exactly why we choose to make decisions in our organisation.

The wide-ranging benefits of pay transparency

With lack of pay transparency and clarity over how and why pay decisions are made, people form their own perceptions about their pay and the pay of their colleagues. The Payscale survey found that two-thirds of employees who were paid the market rate believed they were underpaid. This doesn't have to be the case.

Organisations can implement various degrees of pay transparency – more on this later. Whether it is partial or complete pay transparency, which means disclosing the salaries of all employees, there is plenty of research that shows a clear correlation with increased employee retention.[25] It's only natural, since pay transparency builds trust and any relationship, including a working relationship, lasts longer when it is built on a foundation of trust.

Context about how and why decisions are made enables people to do their jobs more effectively. Transparency allows employees to gain a better understanding of whether their pay is fair by examining the organisation's pay structure, approach to pay and pay progression. This helps them to make more informed choices and negotiate the right salaries. Being able to negotiate effectively with this information to hand is particularly important for women, black and minority ethnic workers who in general tend to be less comfortable negotiating compared to their white male colleagues.

Leaders may argue that in the absence of pay transparency, they are able to negotiate the lowest possible salary for each candidate, helping them to cut costs. Although true, this indicates that the organisation has no interest in ensuring equal pay for its employees. Is that really the sort of organisation you want to work for?

Complete pay transparency at Buffer

Complete transparency and salary disclosure will not work in all organisations. They are more likely to work in organisations where roles are structured and defined, for example, train drivers or warehouse workers. However, some less structured organisations

25   Westbrooks, E, 'Is Salary Transparency the New Key To Employee Retention?', Wrike, www.wrike.com/blog/is-salary-transparency-the-new-key-to-employee-retention, accessed 30 June 2022

do go down this route, and again, research shows a positive correlation with employee retention.

Social media company Buffer implemented a policy of full pay transparency and pay disclosure, publishing the salaries of employees internally as well as for the general public. In 2018, it published employee retention rates of 94%.[26]

Buffer highlights four reasons why it opted for total pay transparency and an all-round transparent culture:

- Buffer realises that transparency breeds trust, which is the foundation of great teamwork. This trust is not just for employees, but customers and anyone the company interacts with. Being open about the reasons and process behind its decisions, the company helps everyone feel informed and on-board.

- Transparency breeds innovation. As Buffer grows and new people join the organisation, new team members need to have all the information to make great decisions.

- Transparency leads to fairness and equity. To have an open system that breeds trust, Buffer has a formula for deciding salaries. That's not to say determining pay is a science; people are different and contribute in various ways, and this needs to be reflected in pay. By having a clear set of criteria and processes, Buffer eliminates inequality and bias when determining salaries.

- Transparency leads to more feedback. When we're transparent about our decision-making process, it leads to

---

26   'State of remote work', *Buffer* (2018), https:/buffer.com/state-of-remote-work/2018, accessed May 2022

additional feedback expressing different points of view. This feedback enables us to continually adjust and improve our process. At Buffer, the feedback was that the formula didn't pay high enough salaries in the San Francisco area. This led the company leaders to review the information and adjust accordingly.

The pay transparency scale

Your approach to pay can be split up into three categories:

1. What do you pay your employees?

2. Why do you manage pay the way you do?

3. How do you make pay decisions?

When we talk about pay transparency, particularly in the media, the focus is usually on *what* everyone is earning, but the fact is, *how* and *why* pay decisions are made is a lot more meaningful to people because they want to know they're being treated fairly and consistently. This was highlighted in the Payscale survey which found that one of the top predictors of employee engagement is an organisation's ability to communicate clearly and honestly about pay.

What does this mean in practice? Think of it in terms of a 1–5 pay transparency scale, shown in the following image. This transparency scale divides the 'what', 'how' and 'why' of pay into five steps, starting with no transparency on the left and moving to complete transparency on the right. This doesn't mean you will necessarily move in a straight line from level 1 to level 5, but if you are looking to increase pay transparency, this scale will help you identify where you are, your destination and how you can get there.

Level 1 is where we know *what* we pay our employees and this is clearly communicated to them. Everyone knows their monthly salary, but do they know the different benefits available to them? Are they aware of the value of those benefits, such as through a total reward statement? This is where almost all organisations start.

Level 2 looks at *why* we manage pay a certain way. What are our reward principles and strategy? What is the purpose of pay? Why should it progress? Is it linked to performance, skills or contribution?

Level 3 is where the *why* is communicated across the organisation, so employees understand the overall reward principles underpinning everything they do. They understand why their pay is managed a certain way.

Level 4 is when we think about *how* we make pay decisions. Some organisations may have an approach to job evaluation and a career framework and pay structure in place, but they are only used within HR and finance.

Level 5 communicates these reward frameworks across the organisation, so employees know *how* pay decisions are made. They know how their role fits into the career framework and how their salary fits into the organisational pay structure. They also know what is expected of them and how their pay will progress as they advance in the organisation.

Not all organisations will move from level 1 to 5. Each organisation is different, but the scale offers a guide for moving towards more pay transparency. It also illustrates that moving towards pay transparency is a gradual process. It is a significant cultural change that requires time, clear communication and stakeholder management. Making a sudden shift without clear communication could do more harm than good.

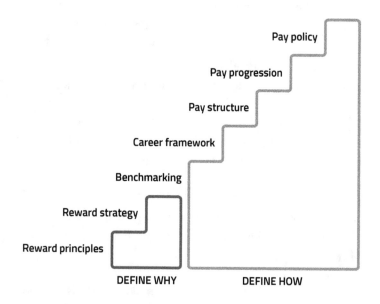

We should all aspire to reach level 5 eventually. Competitor salary data is just a Google search away. Websites like Glassdoor allow people to get a good understanding of market pay rates and this is only going to become more common. If we don't recognise this and instead allow managers to continue making decisions based on 'gut feelings' or keep our pay ranges a secret within HR and finance, then we'll still be talking about 'The Great Resignation' for many years to come.

Now we have looked at the importance of honesty and transparency, treating employees like the intelligent adults they are, how do we decide where to set a base rate for pay within our organisation?

4

Base Pay

'How do you decide the base salary of your employees?'

'I ask people to think about their living expenses, what they consider their essential needs and how much they spend every month to survive. That's my starting point for setting their annual salary.'

This was a real conversation I once had with a CEO. You may think this is bizarre, but the CEO was trying to approach base salary from an ethical point of view. As a leader of a non-profit organisation, they wanted to keep their costs to a minimum so they could spend the funds on projects while ensuring employees had what they needed.

This is problematic on many levels. We could end up paying two people in the same role completely different salaries, based on their expectations and living situation. Is someone who lives with their parents only entitled to a fraction of the salary of someone with a family and a mortgage to pay? This is certainly not going to help the gender or ethnicity pay gap and will create equal pay risks.

The moral of the story is that we can decide base pay for our employees with the best intentions but can still get things wrong if we don't approach it in the right way. Thankfully, the organisation's CEO saw sense and eventually changed their approach.

The purpose of base salary

The first question you need to ask is: what is the purpose of base salary in your organisation? You can't decide how you are going to pay people or make ongoing decisions about pay if you don't know what this purpose is.

Base salary is often based on a combination of factors. It's about getting the right balance between:

Skills and responsibilities. The skills required to carry out a role and the complexity or scope of the role's responsibilities need to impact the salary you offer. For example, if you are looking to hire someone with no previous experience into an administrative role with basic responsibilities, this would result in a much lower salary than if you were looking to recruit someone qualified as an actuary.

Internal equity. This means ensuring similar-level jobs carry a similar salary, so there is equal pay for equal work. This doesn't mean everyone should get paid exactly the same amount, but that, for example, roles of a similar level remain within set pay ranges.

There may be some exceptions, but the vast majority of roles are managed in this way.

External competitiveness. This is about understanding market rates of pay so you can make informed decisions to help you recruit and retain the right people. Don't rely on anecdotal data from recruitment surveys or a couple of slides managers have put together showing competitors' high salaries to negotiate better salaries for themselves or their teams.

As well as knowing market rates of pay, you also need clarity around how you want to position your organisation against the market. Do you want to lead and pay above the market or match it? We'll cover this in more detail in a later chapter.

Individual contribution. This means the contribution someone makes in a role based on their unique skills, knowledge and experience. One person may recently have contributed more than their colleagues due to exceptional performance, but this performance must be ongoing. Exemplary performance on a project or over a single financial year does not necessarily need to be reflected in base salary. How do you define this contribution or performance?

Of course, there are other factors to consider, such as affordability, but that's not the *purpose* of pay. The important thing to remember is that *base pay reflects the ongoing value of a role or individual*. If a salesperson has sold an incredible amount over the last year, that doesn't mean they will continue to do so in the future. It could simply be a result of circumstance or good fortune. It's not an increase in *ongoing* value – and hence a reason for a big pay rise. You may instead choose to provide variable or bonus pay, which is something we will cover later.

Why should pay progress?

Leaders and HR professionals need to be clear about why pay should progress and articulate this to all employees. One conversation I had with a leader went something like this:

'We have a limited budget, so we would like to look at any real concerns or pay increases that are high priority,' said the business lead – let's call him John.

'Actually, there is one person in your team who is significantly underpaid. She's below the market and below peers, so there's also an equal pay risk,' I replied.

'That one is OK. We've looked into it and she's on a work permit and unlikely to leave, so we decided not to make any increases.'

This was early on in my career. Much as I tried to make my case, ultimately it was John's decision. Unfortunately, he was not thinking about what was fair – only about how he could keep his people and hit the organisation's targets for the lowest possible cost. It happened because there were no principles or policies in place to enforce fair pay.

Once you've defined the purpose of base pay in your organisation, the next step is to think about *why* pay should progress. How do you manage your annual pay review process or ad hoc pay increases? What is the governance process?

Here are some of the main reasons pay tends to progress in organisations:

Performance

This has historically been the most common way of progressing pay in the private sector, assuming that current performance = better ongoing contribution to the organisation. Leaders often spend considerable time and resources 'managing' the performance of employees and the outcome (eg performance ratings) decides the pay increase for each person.

There are two challenges with this approach. Firstly, it relies on having a fair and consistent performance management process, which is difficult to monitor, particularly in a large organisation. Secondly, high performance one year may not necessarily lead to high performance in subsequent years, but people are still rewarded with a permanent pay increase.

Length of service

This is more common in the public sector, although some private sector companies continue to reward people based on length of service as well. I won't beat around the bush: this is a bad idea. Say Serena Williams, with twenty-three grand-slam titles to her name, was playing a teenager in the Wimbledon final. Would we give Serena a much better prize for winning, simply because she's been playing longer? That sounds absurd and it is.

Pay progression based purely on length of service, when the employee may only be making the same contribution as their colleagues, is no different. Not to mention the equal pay or age discrimination risks.

Skills and competencies

Many companies progress pay as people develop their competencies. As employees gain new skills, they contribute more to the organisation. For instance, an HR manager typically earns a higher salary than an HR analyst. This is because more skills and competencies are required to fulfil the HR manager role, such as communication, leadership and problem solving.

A significant change in skills or competencies can be measured using a job evaluation process and reflected in pay.

Qualifications

An employee gaining a new qualification or passing exams can also lead to pay progression for them. This may be a formal mechanism or at the discretion of the leaders.

The rationale for increasing pay here is to maintain external competitiveness. It is also indirectly linked to skills and contribution. If someone passes their finance or actuarial exams, they are developing their skills and knowledge, and hence contributing more to the organisation. When they pass their exams, their market value goes up. A part-qualified accountant will demand a significantly higher salary than a finance graduate. If an organisation's pay progression doesn't reflect this, its employees are likely to go elsewhere. However, this doesn't mean that all qualifications should result in a pay increase.

Total contribution

This is my preferred approach, and what we use with our clients at 3R Strategy. Total contribution looks both at input and output, not just what people are accountable for, but their behaviours, development and wider contribution to the team and organisation.

The purpose of this approach is to recognise and reward personal contribution of colleagues in its widest sense and to support their development. It's important to look at behaviours that are aligned to our organisational culture. While many organisations do consider behaviours, there is no clear definition for an employee of what is expected of them, nor for the line manager to be able to make an assessment. There is simply a rating based on the manager's assessment and 'gut feeling'.

Finding the balance

When it comes to pay progression, consider an individual's ongoing value to your organisation. What determines an individual's ongoing value? To a large extent, it is driven by the external market. If most other organisations are paying £50,000 a year to fully qualified accountants, you're going to struggle to recruit anyone for a salary of £30,000. If you currently employ someone at that salary, you will have to increase their pay to get closer to the market, or you will struggle to retain them.

If your organisation cannot afford to pay people a high salary, communicate clearly and honestly to your employees that this is why you choose to pay below the market. You may focus instead on other areas of reward, attracting people due to your organisation's culture or sense of purpose, and then look to increase salaries in the future when it is more profitable.

It's also about striking a balance. You can't give one person a high salary for developing their skills if day-to-day they are still doing the same role and making the same contribution – particularly if colleagues are on much lower salaries. This is an equal pay risk, which we will cover in the next chapter.

Salary benchmarking

We're the Millers is the story of a small-town drug dealer who hires three people to pose as his family so he can transport drugs from Mexico to the US.[27] Jason Sudeikis plays David Clark, the bogus drug-dealing 'dad', and Jennifer Aniston plays Rose O'Reilly, his pretend wife. Casey and Kenny are their pretend children.

The deadline for the drop-off is running out and in a fit of anger, a frustrated David Clark inadvertently reveals to his pretend family how much he's getting paid ($500,000). Rose, incredulous, can't believe that David is making half a million dollars and only giving her $30,000, which then prompts Casey to ask why Rose is getting $30,000 when she is only getting $1,000. Before David has a chance to defend himself, Kenny, the son, pipes up.

'You're all getting paid?'

David had no idea what he should pay these people for helping him to transport drugs while pretending to be his family, so he decided to offer what each of them would find acceptable, resulting in completely different pay for each person.

One of the words I hear often when speaking to leaders is 'unique'. 'Our organisation is unique. The role we need to benchmark is unique.' Therefore, it isn't going to be possible to benchmark a role. There's not going to be any data available. Having worked with hundreds of organisations, they are very rarely unique, although

---

27   Thurber, RM, *We're the Millers* (Warner Bros, 2013)

it's safe to say the roles David Clark was looking to benchmark were pretty unique.

What is salary benchmarking?

Having market intelligence, as well as a good understanding of where your organisation sits in relation to the market, is an essential part of setting an effective reward strategy. This will enable you to recruit new people at the right salary and ensure you are rewarding your existing people appropriately to retain your key talent.

There is a wealth of free information available through recruitment agencies and online forums. Employees are more informed than ever about market rates of pay for their roles. To compete for talent and retain key people in the long run, you must not only develop fair and market-competitive salary ranges, but review them on a regular basis to ensure you are keeping up with the market.

Challenging recruitment salary data

As an HR professional, you are likely to be accustomed to receiving recruitment salary surveys and job adverts from managers challenging your market data, or employees challenging their own salaries. When looking at this information, you need to consider a few factors.

There is a wide range of salaries being advertised on the internet for each role. Employees will inevitably pick out the highest to make their case, so you need to make decisions based on in-depth market research and analysis, rather than anecdotal data from one or two companies – unless you're only recruiting and competing with one or two companies, which is unlikely.

Job adverts and recruitment data tend to show what companies are willing to pay for roles, rather than what they are actually paying. For example, a role may be advertised with a salary of 'up to £50K', but the actual salary offered to the successful candidate may be significantly lower. Alternatively, it may even be higher.

Recruitment and job advert data is not robust and is often based on job titles alone. A finance analyst in one company may be equivalent to a senior finance analyst or a finance manager in another. A good salary survey will look at the content of the roles through a job-evaluation process; in other words, it will consider equivalent *roles* when establishing salary ranges, rather than equivalent job titles. We will go through salary surveys in more detail in a later chapter, as well as how to pick the right salary survey for your organisation.

Getting your salaries right could be the key to attracting and retaining key people in your organisation. Given the potential impact, I highly recommend you research salary survey options and invest in a good data source. Employee costs are usually an organisation's highest expense, so I'm often amazed to find that leaders with hundreds of employees, spending millions on salaries, search for free benchmarks instead of spending a couple of thousand pounds on meaningful data to make informed decisions. When you consider the amount you likely spend on recruitment, training and onboarding per person, this is one of the best investments you and your team can make as an HR function.

When you submit your employee data to a salary survey, the people running the survey often go back to participating organisations with queries to validate their job matching. The full database also goes through a data-cleaning process to ensure the final report is as accurate as possible. Organisations look at the content of each role and match each job to the relevant function and level based on skills and responsibilities. The process relies on the HR team from each organisation completing the survey having a good understanding of their organisation's roles and matching them accurately, so it's important to pick a reliable data source that covers most, if not all, of your roles.

The data is by no means perfect, but your objective is not a formulaic approach linking base salaries to the external market. Rather, the survey offers valuable insight enabling you and your organisation's leaders to make more informed pay decisions.

Understanding market data

The **median salary** represents the mid-point of a data sample. Let's say eleven organisations have a project manager role. If we rank the salaries of these employees from lowest to highest, the organisation that sits in the middle – ranked sixth – has the median salary.

Let's assume that in the following year, two new companies join the survey. There are now thirteen companies with a project manager role. If the new companies pay higher salaries than everyone else, they will be twelfth and thirteenth. Now, the median salary is the seventh salary in the sample.

Even if there have been no pay increases since the previous year, the median salary will have gone up. This is how surveys work: with new companies participating each year and others dropping from the sample, resulting in changes in the data. This is why we shouldn't take a formulaic approach to salary benchmarking, but use it to make sensible pay decisions.

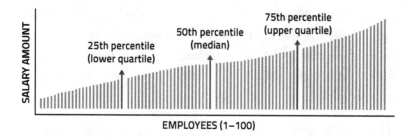

Quartiles and deciles. Most salary surveys publish lower (25th percentile) and upper (75th percentile) quartiles, as well as the market median. The best way to think about this is to imagine a data set of 100 employees, each with a unique salary. These salaries are placed in order from lowest to highest.

The 25th highest salary in the sample (25th percentile) is known as the lower quartile (LQ). The 75th highest salary (75th percentile) is known as the upper quartile (UQ). In other words, quartiles sort data into four quarters. Some surveys may also publish deciles to give you more insight into market salaries. Deciles sort data into ten equal parts. The 10th highest salary (10th percentile) is the 1st decile. The 90th highest salary (90th percentile) is the 9th decile.

Now that you have an understanding of the purpose behind base salary for your organisation and an idea of how to work out the ideal base salary for each role within that organisation, it's time to have a closer look at pay benchmarking and starting salaries.

5

Pay Benchmarking And Starting Salaries

Before you benchmark your organisation's roles against the external market, you need to have a benchmarking strategy. Are you going to position your organisation against the market median? Do you want to lead the market with aggressive growth and recruit the best people by paying closer to the UQ? Some leaders choose to invest in other areas or feel they have a strong enough brand to attract talent, so position their salaries below the market at the LQ. You can even use a market median reference for the majority of your roles, but position yourself at the higher end of the market for a few critical and highly technical roles.

There are other reasons you may choose to pay below the market. When I first set up my pay consultancy, 3R Strategy, I didn't have a business partner or any investment. All of the income the business generated was reinvested to help it grow. As a result, I couldn't afford to pay salaries at the market median and positioned my business around the LQ.

I discussed this with my team with the understanding that as the business grew, we could afford to position our pay rates more highly against the market. During that transition, no one left the organisation, which was able to grow considerably. This to me proves the positive impact of a clear strategy that is communicated to all employees, even if you are paying below the market.

Whatever you decide, you need to apply a clear strategy consistently across the organisation. The benchmark data you use can be a critical part of your annual pay review when the salaries of your employees are likely to progress. This is often a complex process that needs to be managed effectively.

Benchmarking in the age of remote working

In early 2020, I was giving a presentation to the senior management team of a company on a new reward strategy. Towards the end of the presentation, I talked about introducing a flexible working policy. Although HR is always supportive of this, I could see a few other people rolling their eyes.

The organisation already had a flexible working policy. If people wanted to come in at 9.30am instead of 9am, they could get approval for a change in their working pattern. Working from home was not something the leaders felt would be beneficial for their organisation. I explained that being able to change their working pattern by half an hour isn't really 'flexible working' in the eyes of most people, particularly Millennials and Generation Z, but the recommendation didn't progress much further.

A few weeks later, everyone in the company and most people around the world were working from home and would continue to do so for the rest of the year. There was certainly an accelerated change in mindset as a result of the COVID-19 pandemic; I say 'accelerated' because the huge increase in remote working probably would have happened anyway.

Working from Home

Prior to 2020, there was already a significant portion of the workforce seeking out roles and organisations that allowed flexibility and did not undermine their family life. This group has grown exponentially since the pandemic. As the competition for talent increases, organisations can no longer afford to be rigid in their approach to how employees work.

It wasn't just employees that were impacted by the pandemic. Many businesses, particularly in the hospitality sector, went bankrupt and stopped trading. Therefore, it is no surprise that companies looked for other ways to cut costs.

Many organisations asked employees to take a temporary voluntary pay cut due to the difficult market conditions. This is a fair request in times of extreme hardship, such as a worldwide pandemic, particularly when it is a choice between redundancy for some colleagues or a temporary pay cut for everyone. I speak from experience because this is something I accepted many years ago during a recession. The question we as HR professionals need to ask is whether this is necessary for the survival of the company or simply a way to achieve arbitrary targets so the CEO and board can get their massive bonuses – more on this later in the chapter.

Should home workers be paid less?

A question some leaders asked at the start of the pandemic was: should employees take a pay cut now that many of them work remotely? After all, by working from home, they save money on transport and day-to-day expenses. I was asked this exact question by the CEO of a potential client organisation who was looking to do a reward review. I'm sure it didn't help my proposal, but I explained why this was an awful idea and I wouldn't recommend that any company does this. Here's why.

When my 3R Strategy team and I conduct salary benchmarking for our clients, I always ask where the client recruits from and where people go when they leave. Are they recruiting locally or from a much wider geographical area? Location and industry play a decisive role in salary benchmarking, and while some may benchmark against national data, others might look to regional or even city-specific figures.

Where does this leave us post-pandemic when remote working has become a way of life for a large proportion of the workforce? The pandemic has shown that working remotely at scale is both achievable and, for many employees, desirable on a more permanent basis – which means employees could reasonably live anywhere.

It seems increasingly likely that in the future, organisations will stop looking at local data altogether, opting instead for national data, with the possible exception of organisations based in areas like Central London that require employees to come in to the workplace. For the most part, this is good news. National data offers a robust sample size compared to regional data, which can be less reliable and more likely to fluctuate from year to year.

In the vast majority of cases, leaders will be better served by looking at the national data, but this only makes sense if organisations are not demanding that their employees come into the office every day. Of course, there will always be some roles that cannot be carried out remotely and hence need to be filled from the local talent market.

Back to the question of whether we should pay people a lower salary if they no longer pay travel costs or buy lunch and coffee in the office every day. It's important we think back to the previous chapter and ask why we pay a base salary in the first place. Is it to reflect our employees' skills and contributions, or is it merely a reflection of their living standards and expenses? By that rationale, we would expect to pay the employee who lives in Central London and drives a Mercedes a much higher salary than the employee who lives outside the city centre and rides a bicycle, because their living standards and expenses would be much higher.

The fact is if two people are doing the same job, lifestyle is irrelevant. Whether they commute in to work or not is irrelevant. Whether they buy lunch and a latte every day is irrelevant. When we used to require everyone to come into the office to work, did we ask people where they lived or how much they were spending on commuting and adjust salaries accordingly? These factors should not be part of our decision making. Yes, we can choose to pay at the LQ because that's what we can afford, but that policy should apply to all employees, regardless of their life choices.

This also links back to your employees' right to equal pay for equal work. This being the case, there is no justification for reducing salaries just because employees have stopped buying train tickets and save money on Pret sandwiches.

Finally, consider the counterargument. Since employees are no longer coming in to work, they may point out that the company is saving money by using less office space. Does this mean employees are justified in asking for a higher salary? What about companies like Google that provide meals to all its employees at the office? If employees are no longer coming into the office, this is a cost saving for the organisation.

Ultimately, paying remote workers less than those who come into the office has been used as an excuse by a small minority of companies to reduce costs. While some organisations were contemplating reducing salaries in 2020, the narrative changed completely in 2021 with 'The Great Resignation'. Suddenly, companies were struggling to recruit and retain people, having to offer much higher salaries rather than make any reductions. These responses highlight the need for a clear strategy and principles so we're not always reacting to short-term market trends and creating possible equal pay risks in our organisations.

Managing your annual pay review process

'The executive team wants to ask employees to delay their pay review for six months. In return, the entire executive team will delay their pay review for a whole year,' I was told by one leader.

'That's nice of them. I'm sure people will appreciate that. What will you achieve by delaying pay review by six months?'

'We'll save around £2 million, which will enable us to hit our annual targets.'

'What happens if you hit your targets?'

'The executive team will all get their bonuses.' The CEO was on a bonus of 100% of base salary, so they would barely notice not accepting a small pay increase.

This, another real conversation I had with a private sector leader, is a lesson in how *not* to manage pay review. Pay review is a regular occurrence that impacts all your people; it's important that you clearly articulate your purpose and process.

Defining your purpose

In some smaller organisations, there are no formal company-wide pay reviews; pay rises are awarded on an individually negotiated basis. However, most organisations conduct pay reviews once per year, across the whole business.

Having a pay review doesn't necessarily mean everyone will receive a pay increase, but it does mean that all salaries will be considered. Before putting together a pay review process, you must first establish your objectives. This is particularly important if HR has given leaders responsibility for making pay decisions.

For instance, is the purpose of the pay review to recognise exceptional performance over the previous year? Is it to reflect individuals' skills and contributions? Is it to keep up with cost-of-living increases? Do you want to ensure that there is internal equity or is the focus to align salaries with the external market?

In addition, you need to establish who is eligible for a pay increase. Is everyone eligible or are new starters excluded? What about people who have been recently promoted and already received a pay increase? Start by putting together a pay policy detailing how you will manage pay for all your employees in your review process.

Many leaders take a formulaic approach to the pay review process. They look at distribution curves and allocate fixed pay increases to people based on their rating. As we've previously discussed, this approach is problematic for many reasons, including for the annual pay review.

The starting point is usually a forced distribution of ratings or a calibration that indirectly leads to 'normal' distribution. We will discuss this in more detail in Chapter 10, including why forced distribution is a terrible idea. For pay review, it leads to a situation where employees are essentially competing with each other for a higher pay increase. Is that what you want to drive in your organisation? Employees competing with each other rather than collaborating?

Many organisations provide different pay increases to employees based on their performance or other factors. With pay review budgets being relatively low in recent years, there is little differentiation possible through this approach. For example, a pay review budget of 2% may allow the highest performers to get a 4% pay increase compared to a 'good' or 'average' performer at 1%, but there may be a significant difference in what the high performers are contributing. It would be like Manchester United giving Cristiano Ronaldo a 4% pay increase compared to 1.5% for

Jonathan Greening. Jonathan who? Exactly! Ronaldo would just go and play for another team.

This approach does not consider market data. Let's say you have an employee who has been with you for many years and has been promoted into a finance manager role. You have also recruited a new candidate into another finance manager role. As is often the case, the new employee is on a higher salary as they are more familiar with market rates, having interviewed for several jobs.

Let's assume these two people are making a similar contribution in their roles, but the formulaic approach to annual pay review does not allow you to bridge this salary gap. Either you have to do this with an out-of-cycle pay increase or loyal employees lose out by not having an opportunity to catch up to the market.

By making fixed pay increases, we are unable to address any equal pay concerns. If two employees (one male and one female) are in the same role on vastly different salaries, despite having similar skills and making a similar contribution, this would be an equal pay concern. By only linking pay increases to performance ratings, we are unable to make any adjustments for equal pay discrepancies as part of our regular pay review process.

Starting salaries

Recruitment agencies and many in-house recruitment teams ask candidates what their previous salary was. What is the purpose of asking this question? It's usually one of two reasons:

1. To help determine what salary to offer the candidate. In my experience, in the vast majority of cases, this is the reason recruitment teams and line managers ask about current salaries.

2. A lazy way to ascertain the value of a candidate and their skills/qualifications. If that is the purpose, then a better way to determine this would be to look at the candidate's CV and work experience.

If #1 is the reason we're asking about a candidate's current salary, then this is problematic. The question should be banned. What if the candidate is paid unfairly in their current role? Perhaps that is the reason they decided to search for a new role, meaning we are using flawed data to determine the future salaries and livelihoods of our colleagues. Women, people of colour or those with disabilities who may have faced pay discrimination all their lives simply transfer this inequity from one organisation to another when we ask this question.

Imagine employee A and employee B have the same knowledge and skills and are doing the same job with a market rate of £50,000. Employee A is on a salary of £30,000, while employee B is on a salary of £50,000.

Employee A complains and finally decides to move to another company. The new company's HR team asks for their current salary and decides that a £20K pay increase is too much, so offers a salary of £40,000. This is a big (£10K and 33%) pay rise, but still an equal pay risk. It is wrong to pay this new employee a lower salary than others doing the same job in the organisation. All this does is transfer pay discrimination and inequity from one organisation to another.

If we're going to promote equal pay, we have to offer a salary based on the role and the candidate's skills and experience. If we accept that some pay inequalities exist, whether they are due to gender, ethnicity or any other factor, then why would we want to use this data to make future pay decisions?

To make sure we don't let this flawed information influence our pay decisions, we must stop asking candidates for their existing salaries. In fact, many states in the USA have banned this question from the recruitment process. Whether this becomes law or not, let's just ban it in our organisations too and make pay decisions based only on how roles are evaluated (more on this in the next chapter) and the skills and experience of the candidate.

If you have been asked this question during a recruitment process and not known how to respond, I've put together some guidance. Go to 3r-strategy.com/why-we-need-to-stop-asking-about-current-salary

With a strong benchmarking strategy in place and a good idea of how to and how *not* to calculate a candidate's starting salary with your organisation, we're now ready to take a look at your employees' career and pay progression.

6

Career And Pay Progression

Imagine you have a senior finance manager in your organisation, responsible for financial planning, budgets and reporting. She is on a salary of £60,000 a year, but feels she is underpaid for her role, so she decides to do some online research.

She emails you several links for senior finance manager roles in other organisations offering considerably higher salaries and finds a recruitment salary survey, which lists a salary range for senior finance managers from £80,000 to £90,000. So far, it seems like a compelling case for a pay increase.

Scenarios like this have been commonplace since… well, since Google was invented, but just because these examples have the same job title doesn't mean they're actually the same job. Your organisation may just have a different approach to job titles; your senior finance manager may be performing the same role as a finance manager at most other organisations.

Job titles can be misleading. How many of us know a 'manager' who has listed themselves as a 'director' on their LinkedIn profile? This is where job evaluation comes in.

Job evaluation

This is a systematic way of assessing the skills and responsibilities of a role objectively. Most pay and reward activities rely on organisations having a robust job evaluation process in place.

A job evaluation process:

- Provides a foundation for having a fair pay and career framework

- Provides a basis for evaluating the role – not the job holder or employee

- Helps you understand the comparative relationship between roles

- Allows you to benchmark your pay externally against other organisations

- Enables you to ensure you are providing equal pay for equal work

When we think about job evaluation, many of us think about complex points-factor systems that require a significant amount of training and, in some cases, even a certification. There is also a perception that job evaluation processes are costly and difficult to maintain, but there are many types and they do not need to be so complex.

The image shows the simplest type of job evaluation to the left, where you rank jobs based on their hierarchy in the organisation. Over to the right, you have the more complex point-factor-based approach, which considers a number of factors for each job and assigns points for each one. The overall average, or weighted average, results in the evaluation for the role.

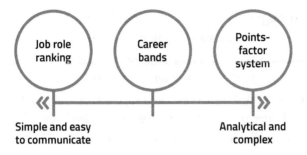

Job ranking system

This is the simplest form of job evaluation and requires little time and investment. In this system, each job is ranked according to its importance within the organisation. For example, your first-ranked job will be the CEO and the second-ranked will be all of their direct reports.

Due to its simplicity, it is not very sophisticated and doesn't tell you much about the difference between roles. All you know is that one is ranked higher than the other.

Points-factor system

A much more complex way of evaluating roles is a points-factor system such as the Hay job evaluation method,[28] which is commonly used in the public sector. A points-factor system looks at things such as problem solving and communication and defines them at varying levels of complexity to demonstrate progression of roles. The factors may have equal weighting, or each can be weighted differently to give an overall evaluation for each role.

---

28   'Job Evaluation: Foundations and applications', Korn Ferry, www.kornferry.com/content/dam/kornferry/docs/pdfs/job-evaluation.pdf, accessed 29 June 2022

This process provides a deep analysis of the roles and is typically more consistent and accurate than the other methods. It is the most robust way of ensuring that roles of 'equal value' or 'rated as equivalent' under the Equality Act 2010 (UK) are evaluated correctly. However, it also requires a lot of time and resources to manage. Large organisations using this method often invest in a technology solution to support the process.

Career bands

Career bands or levels represent roles according to the skills and responsibilities required, regardless of job function or job family. These skills can either be defined at a generic level or a set of 'impact factors' (such as accountability, autonomy, communication, etc) can be defined for each career band. The level of skill and responsibility gets more complex as you move to higher career bands. This gives the simplicity of the job ranking approach, but adds some sophistication through clear definitions for each band, providing a fair and consistent approach to job evaluation.

As with most things, there is no right or wrong answer, as each organisation is different. In general, if you're using narrow bands, you are likely to need a more robust job evaluation process, whereas with broader bands, you can take a more flexible and simpler approach. There'll be more on narrow vs broad bands later in the chapter.

Maybe you have seen the film *Taken* with Liam Neeson.[29] Even if you haven't, you may know of the famous scene where he makes a threatening phone call to the people who have kidnapped his daughter.

---

29   Morel, P, *Taken* (20th Century Studios, 2008)

Liam Neeson's character tells the kidnappers that he doesn't have the ransom money that they're asking for. What he does have are skills – skills acquired over a long career that mean he could become the kidnappers' worst nightmare. Here's a man who takes job evaluation seriously and has clearly evaluated his own role.

Job evaluation is the solid foundation of a reward project. Before you can begin to build any kind of structure, you need to lay this solid foundation.

There are many other benefits of having a job evaluation framework that you can use in your organisation. In the next section, though, we will focus on career frameworks and pathways.

Picking the right career path

Derek Zoolander is based on a character Ben Stiller created for a VH1 fashion show in 1996.[30] It pokes fun at and exaggerates the vanity paraded about in the fashion industry and the stereotype that models are dumb. In fact, Ben Stiller and Owen Wilson remind us many times during the film just how dumb they are.

Derek Zoolander finds that his career is going downhill after he fails to win Male Model of the Year for the fourth year in a row, thanks to his rival Hansel. Why is this so important to Zoolander? In an interview with a reporter, he describes catching his reflection in a spoon during second grade and thinking himself so attractive that he 'could make a career out of being "professionally good-looking"'. What Zoolander needed was a meeting with HR to develop a more thoughtful approach to his long-term career options.

---

30   Stiller, B, *Zoolander* (Paramount Picture, 2001)

A career conversation

What is a career framework?

A career framework allows leaders to make more informed pay and reward decisions when it comes to many HR processes such as pay, including equal pay, reward or promotions. It also enables them to be more organised and have better insight about the skills available in their organisation, allowing them to be strategic with succession planning so that if employees leave critical roles, there are other people with similar skills who are able to step in.

Leaders of small organisations tend to make decisions according to the whims of their managers, but the bigger the company, the harder it is to ensure these decisions are consistent – especially for those organisations that operate across different sectors and/or multiple countries. This is where a career framework allows you to have a holistic view across the organisation, establishing a clear system for managing pay, benefits and career progression while ensuring consistency in decision making.

Say you have a number of levels or career bands (or whatever you decide to call them), each level defined by a particular set of skills and responsibilities. The skills described at each level increase in complexity as you move to a higher level or band.

With a career framework in place, there are various other processes that you can develop and implement. Job levelling or banding sets the foundation for activities like learning and development – for instance, what does it take to move someone from one level to another? You can then tailor training programmes around the knowledge and skills needed for career progression.

Each level or band typically has a broad definition that applies to all types of roles in the organisation, eg HR, finance and IT. This can be a few sentences describing wide-ranging skills or a bit more detailed with specific factors such as 'communication' or 'problem solving' for each level/band. This is similar to having your own framework to evaluate roles against your organisational factors to find the right level/band for each role. What's more, having a career framework enables you to look to the external market for salary data, allowing you to create salary benchmarks for roles that require similar skills.

When you have a career framework, each role is evaluated and placed into one of your career bands or levels. Each level/band has a pay range around it to enable you to manage pay more effectively. From here, you can reward everyone consistently, according to their skills and responsibilities. You are now making informed decisions.

What about people who have similar skills and responsibilities, but are making vastly different contributions to the business? Shouldn't they be on different salaries?

Yes, there certainly can be different salaries. Having a career framework doesn't mean everyone is on exactly the same salary, but if there are differences in contribution, you need to understand why those differences exist and identify cases where they are not warranted.

A common language for HR professionals

HR teams are always looking for more efficient ways to administer their programmes and policies in their organisation. A job levelling framework forms the cornerstone for streamlining analysis and decision making, as well as giving an overview of the organisation as a whole. Job levelling solves one of the most common challenges HR leaders face: the ability to compare the value of work and make decisions in a consistent and comprehensive way.

Using a standard job evaluation methodology, HR teams can form a common language to describe career pathways, job requirements and performance expectations.

Narrow vs broad bands

Some organisations are hierarchical and have many narrow job levels or grades. Others can have much broader bands which allow them more flexibility.

Narrow bands are made up of a large number of grades which can vary depending on the size of the organisation. This type of structure is often found in the public sector or where roles are more defined. In some of these organisations, pay progression is determined by specific increases which were historically based on length of service. This was considered the fairest way to determine pay, but there are a few issues with this approach.

- From the organisation's perspective, regardless of whether employees are carrying out their responsibilities and contributing to the organisation, they continue to receive a pay increase.

- There are concerns around age discrimination and equal pay. If two employees do the same job with the same skills and responsibilities, one could be on a considerably higher salary simply because they've been present in the role much longer.

- With narrow bands, there is a danger of what we call in HR 'grade creep'. Narrow bands allow little flexibility and as employees reach the top of the band, they demand higher pay. The only way for leaders to allow this is by moving the employee to a higher grade, but not because they have developed their skills or increased their contribution. This undermines consistency and fairness in the process.

There are also advantages to having narrow bands:

- They give employees a much clearer vision of their career path and how they need to progress to the next grade or step.

- The narrow bands make it easy for leaders to manage their budgets and costs if salaries cannot go higher than the maximum of the range.

- With narrow bands, there are more frequent promotions for employees if they develop their skills and increase their contributions.

With broad bands, there are fewer levels in the organisation and broader descriptions for each band, allowing more flexibility for changes in roles and responsibilities, as well as salaries, without always having to re-evaluate roles. Broad bands are more prevalent in sectors or organisations that need more flexibility, such as financial services.

The potential issues with broad bands are:

- They require a lot more communication and education so managers and employees can have meaningful conversations. As the bands and salary ranges are wide, there are no visible promotions and employees can feel that over long periods of time, they don't have enough meaningful career progression.

- They have wide pay ranges, which means there is more work for the HR team to manage and understand the pay differences that exist for roles within the same band. This means benchmarking more roles to decide where to place them within the wide pay range.

- Broad bands and pay ranges make it more difficult for the organisation to control costs. With narrow bands, employees can only get to the top of their grades, but there is much more scope for pay progression within the broader bands. This also makes it more difficult for leaders to understand and identify equal pay risks.

The advantages of broad bands are:

- They reflect the fact that the organisation isn't hierarchical. Roles and responsibilities in many modern organisations are more fluid than they used to be and broad bands allow these changes without HR having to constantly evaluate roles to establish a new grade. The focus is on the development of skills and growth rather than traditional hierarchical promotion to a new grade.

- They result in wider pay ranges which allow more flexibility for leaders to manage pay. If you are looking to recruit an exceptional candidate who could add a great deal of value to your organisation, but is seeking a higher than average or median salary, you could manage this with a broad pay range, whereas you may lose out to a competitor if your pay · range doesn't allow this flexibility.

- With broad bands, there is a much greater focus on the development of skills, lateral movement within the organisation and retention of employees instead of a constant race to the top. Broad bands are also more likely to be linked with competencies that lead to success in the role and within the organisation. This is something we will explore in more detail in the next chapter.

As you can see, there are pros and cons to both types of career frameworks, and as with most things, there isn't a right or wrong answer. What is your objective in introducing job levels or a career framework? Which framework is more suited to your organisational objectives and culture? We will explore this in more detail in Part Three.

Developing career path visibility

Increasingly, the world of work is focusing less on hierarchical structures and more on skills, capabilities and experiences. Employers will need to show clear career progression opportunities to attract and retain talent.

A job levelling framework can help you respond to what your employees are asking for, setting clear expectations and career-path visibility. Employees want to know where they stand within an organisation and how they can progress. Job levelling offers an explicit route forward, so employees can aspire to their next role.

Career development and progression have been hot topics for a long time. In organisations with little opportunity for career progression, high performers will often choose to leave – much to the detriment of the business – so how can your organisation make the most of career pathways to hold on to your best employees?

Career pathways are used to identify and support employee development opportunities, as well as to address the capabilities required to support an organisation's business strategy. Historically, career pathways have been defined as vertical progression within a structured hierarchy of roles, each step up carrying more responsibility. With today's changing workforce, career pathways are evolving into a series of developmental opportunities offering various forms of career movement, both vertical and lateral, to encompass new skills, experiences and perspectives.

Career ladders

- Hierarchical structure
- Linear vertical career paths
- No distinction between technical and people management skills

Career pathways

- Flatter matrix structure
- Dual career paths
- Focus on growth and development rather than vertical progression

Dual career paths and undesirable leadership

Increasingly, leaders are taking a different approach: identifying *dual career paths* that distinguish between individual contributors and roles that require people-management skills.

Organisations tend to recruit people for their particular skills and capabilities, and if they perform well, they are promoted. As individuals move up the career ladder, they may find themselves managing a team. These decisions are often made because people are good at their jobs – not necessarily because they have good leadership or people-management skills.

Forcing individuals into leadership roles alienates two groups of people:

- Employees who have no desire to take on people-management responsibility, but see it as the only route to progression.

- High performers who are technically skilled, but lack emotional intelligence and the ability to manage others.

Not Everyone Wants to be a Manager

To tackle this conundrum, the dual career path approach enables leaders to provide alternatives to their employees. Of course, it isn't always possible to offer alternatives and there will be times when progression in a particular function requires taking on people-management responsibility. In this case, it is vital that your organisation offers leadership training to anyone being given people-management responsibility.

Preferably, make this training a prerequisite before anyone is given people-management responsibility. A new manager with no desire or aptitude can do plenty of damage to the morale of the entire team in a just few months if they haven't been given any guidance. In this case, it may be better to defer people-management responsibilities to another senior manager in the interim.

Being clear about career progression

Whether your organisation develops dual career paths or shifts focus to offer more developmental opportunities, it's important to have a clear career planning strategy:

- Defining behaviours – not just 'what', but 'how'

- Emphasising long-term organisational fit vs short-term need

- Providing employees with clarity around career-development opportunities

- Ensuring that anyone placed in a people-management role is given adequate support and leadership training before they start

Career progression doesn't always mean moving into a more senior role, but it could mean taking on larger, more challenging projects. Employees want to see what the future holds. If they decide to stay loyal to your organisation, where could they see themselves in the future? What you don't want is for your employees to get more clarity over their careers from looking at their reflection in a spoon than from their HR department.

A transparent career framework allows employees to picture and plan their long-term career with your organisation. This doesn't mean there will always be a development or promotion opportunity available, but all of the opportunities – or lack of them – will be clearly visible. Lack of career progression is one of the main reasons why people leave their role to join another organisation, so giving people clarity over this is invaluable.

A career framework built around a sound job evaluation process gives HR and all employees a clear understanding of the skills and responsibilities at different levels within the organisation, and how they need to develop those skills to progress. Performance and contribution aren't just demonstrated by what we do, but how we do it – that is, the behaviours we demonstrate in our role. Behaviours at work are important because collectively, they define our organisational culture.

How do employees know which behaviours are important to your organisation and how to demonstrate them? These are the behavioural competencies that we will discuss in the next chapter.

7

Behavioural Competencies

Lieutenant Colonel Frank Slade, played by Al Pacino in the film *Scent of a Woman*,[31] is an intense and bitter military veteran who lost his sight late in life. Charlie Simms, played by a young Chris O'Donnell, needs to make some extra money and decides to take care of Colonel Slade over the Thanksgiving break.

Charlie is expecting to spend a weekend in the cottage where Colonel Slade lives while his niece is out of town, but Slade has other ideas. He buys tickets to New York, where their adventure begins. They go to a hotel ballroom, Colonel Slade drives a Ferrari, and Charlie manages to save the Colonel from committing suicide in his hotel room, which seems to have been his plan all along.

In the background is Charlie's trouble at school. He and another student, George, witnessed some children playing a practical joke on the headmaster. Charlie and George know who did it, but lie that they did not get a good look at the prankster. Charlie is even bribed by the headmaster with admission to Harvard if he cooperates. George eventually comes clean, under pressure from his father, but Charlie can't bring himself to be a snitch. This is where Colonel Slade delivers a masterful monologue in support of

---

31   Brest, M, *Scent of a Woman* (City Light Films, 1992)

Charlie, who could quite easily take the easy way out and not be expelled from school.

Colonel Slade describes how throughout his life, he always knew what the right path was, but never took it because it was too hard. Yet Charlie has chosen a path of principle that will lead to character, and Slade implores the school committee to see this and consider Charlie's future.

Choices are influenced by beliefs

I watched *Scent of a Woman* when I was quite young and it's a film that had a huge impact on me as a person. Even as a twelve-year-old, I knew that Colonel Slade's was a powerful speech with a deep, profound meaning. I remember listening to that monologue over and over again, trying to comprehend the full meaning of it.

There is ambiguity over whether Charlie's actions were right or wrong, Colonel Slade says so himself, but there is no ambiguity over his integrity. Charlie has strong ethical standards and values and, regardless of the consequences, he sticks to them.

The lesson here is that we will all experience difficult situations in our lives and have to make tough choices. There's no way of knowing whether we are always making the right choices, but what's more important is why we have chosen a particular path. What beliefs and convictions led to those choices?

In the workplace, the way we expect our colleagues to behave and the standards we require are defined by our values, which are articulated clearly through behavioural competencies.

Why we need behavioural competencies

The most important things for an organisation are its vision and values. Where is your organisation striving to get to and how do you want to get it there?

Once you have answers to these questions, you need people with the right knowledge and skills to help you get there, but how do you know whether these people are aligned to your organisational vision and values? It's fine to claim to have values of integrity and trust – but how do you know these really exist within your recruits?

Competencies are different from the responsibilities listed in a job description or a job evaluation process, which focus on what people are required to do. Behavioural competencies define *how* we expect them to do this.

For example, the responsibility listed on a job description could be around delivering presentations to clients. How can we know which candidates would do well in this task? The competency we would look for is being customer oriented. This means being able to provide good customer service, listening to customer feedback and building strong, personalised relationships with the customers.

Expressing all of this in behavioural terms is important, so we define competencies necessary for successful performance within our organisation and provide examples of how to show those behaviours.

In Part One of the book, we discussed the importance of building the right culture in your organisation. To do this, you need to define your organisational values. For example, your values may include innovation or trust, but what does this really mean for employees? What behaviours do they need to demonstrate in their day-to-day activities that will help build this culture of trust and innovation? We clarify this through behavioural competencies.

There are many benefits to having competencies in your organisation, which include:

Recruitment

- Recruit and retain people who share our organisational values and capabilities, which lead to exceptional performance and career fulfilment

- Increase our likelihood of hiring people who will succeed in the job

- Ensure a more consistent approach to recruitment by asking relevant questions to all candidates

- Reduce the time investment needed by HR and managers by only interviewing those candidates that are likely to align with our desired competencies

Performance Management

- Provide a common understanding of what is required to be successful in the organisation, and a clear way to measure this

- Support meaningful conversations between managers and their team to help growth and development

- Understand if employees are achieving their objectives as well as demonstrating the company's 'desired behaviours'

- Create a common language, aligned to the company's values, to clearly identify what is expected of employees to enable them to carry out their roles effectively

- Help managers to be objective when assessing performance

Training and Development

- Develop learning and development opportunities for our people aligned to our organisational values

- Enable employees to focus on the skills and behaviours that have the most impact in their roles

- Provide a framework for ongoing coaching and feedback

Succession Planning

- Recognise and promote the employees who demonstrate, and continue to develop, capabilities and behaviours aligned to our organisational strategy

- Provide a framework for understanding whether candidates are ready to take on a particular role

- Allow us to gauge which employees have the capability to take on more responsibility, and any potential skills gaps

What does all this have to do with pay? Increasingly, pay is not just linked to what we do in the workplace, but how we do it. More and more organisations evaluate their employees annually, looking at both the 'what' and the 'how', but while objectives are typically set for employees, there is often little clarity over the 'how'. If we are going to continue to emphasise 'how' we achieve our objectives – which we should – then we need to make a greater effort to provide our employees with clarity. We may have a value of 'showing integrity', but how does an employee demonstrate integrity in the workplace on a day-to-day basis as part of their role? We need to define this clearly. This is where behavioural competencies come in.

Now that we've looked at pay, pay progression and how it is linked to skills and behaviours, let's delve into the topic of equal pay; a legal requirement, and the universal concept of fair pay.

8

Equal Pay And Fair Pay

There is a subtle difference between equal pay and fair pay. Where equal pay is a legal requirement relating to the Equality Act 2010 (UK), the concept of fair pay is universal and linked to social responsibility. Let's have a closer look at each one.

What is equal pay?

According to the UK Equality Act 2010,[32] men and women doing 'equal work' must receive equal pay unless the difference can be justified. Equal work under this Equality Act is:

- 'Like work' – the same or broadly similar work involving similar tasks and responsibilities

- 'Work rated as equivalent' – using a job evaluation scheme

- 'Work of equal value' – where work is different, but of equal value in terms of the demands of the role

I know that sounds confusing and legal language often is, but what does this really mean for an HR professional? Let's break it down.

---

32   'Equality Act 2010', Legislation.gov.uk,
www.legislation.gov.uk/ukpga/2010/15/notes/division/3/5/3/2, accessed May 2022

Like work

This implies that employees are doing work that is the same or broadly similar. Up-to-date job descriptions can help establish which work is similar and if there are any differences of practical importance. If you have hundreds or thousands of jobs in your organisation, doing an analysis by job title can be a good starting point, but be careful because inconsistencies in job titles are a big frustration for HR teams. If your job titles are up to date and accurate, this is a good way to identify like work.

An example of like work can be men and women working in a supermarket doing a similar role, but the men are occasionally required to lift heavier items. As this is a minor difference, the two roles will still be considered like work.

Work rated as equivalent

This is based on a job evaluation process. If your organisation has a job level or career framework where you place roles based on their skills and responsibilities, this is how you identify work rated as equivalent. The job evaluation scheme should look at the demands of the role and various components (eg the level of skills and knowledge it requires), not just the overall content.

An example of work rated as equivalent is the famous case at Asda where the shop workers (mainly women) were considered comparable to the warehouse and distribution roles (mainly performed by men).[33]

---

33   Ihnatowicz, N, 'Asda Equal Pay Case: Court of Appeal Decision', The HR Director (12 April 2021), www.thehrdirector.com/legal-updates/legal-updates-2021/supermarket-retail-staff-can-compare-their-terms-to-those-of-distribution-workers-in-asda-equal-pay-case-supreme-court-upholds-court-of-appeal-decision, accessed 30 June 2022

Work of equal value

This applies to roles that are different, but of equal value in terms of the demands of the job (skills, knowledge, effort and responsibilities). This is relevant in the absence of a job evaluation scheme or when the scheme undervalues demands that are typically carried out by women. An example of a job that has been ruled to be of equal value by the courts is a school nursery nurse (typically carried out by women) equal to a local government architectural technician (typically carried out by men).[34]

If you have an analytical job evaluation scheme in place that considers the skills, knowledge and responsibilities of each role, then you should be able to establish which are of equal value and equivalent.

Equal pay does *not* mean that everyone should be paid exactly the same salary for doing similar roles. You wouldn't pay a finance manager based in Central London, for example, the same salary as a finance manager based in Lisburn, Northern Ireland. You would either make the employee in Lisburn very happy with a high salary or lose your employee in Central London because of a low salary. Also, if you have two people in a sales role with one bringing in £100,000 of revenue a year and the other bringing in £1,000,000 of revenue, you wouldn't want to reward them in the same way.

If pay differences for similar roles exist, you need to be clear about why this is. Such differences in pay will be considered lawful if there is a genuine reason not related to sex discrimination. This reason could be, for example, a skills shortage, roles that have unsociable hours or geographical differences in pay.

34   'Equal Work', Equality and Human Rights Commission, www.equalityhumanrights.com/en/advice-and-guidance/equal-work, accessed 29 June 2022

What is fair pay?

The definition of equal pay may differ from country to country, but there is a universal understanding of fair pay, which is linked to our social responsibility. This means to:

- Provide consistency in decision making for roles with a similar level of skills and competencies
- Provide employees with a fair living wage
- Assess the relationship between employee and executive pay
- Understand and eliminate pay gaps linked to gender or other demographics, such as race and religion

How do we do this from an HR perspective? There are two things we need to look out for:

- Fairness in our processes – these are our policies and practices. For example, how is pay determined when a new employee is hired? Do we have a pay structure or a career framework?

- Fairness in outcomes – how is our pay budget distributed and do we analyse the data? Can this lead to unfair practices? How is performance measured? How are promotions granted? Have we analysed our data to see if there are some undesired trends emerging?

Why have fair pay?

The running theme of this book is transparency. To be transparent, we first need to be fair. This builds trust and shows our employees that we value and respect them because we share our principles and processes with them.

Fairness and transparency have several benefits:

- Increasing employee engagement and commitment

- Enhancing our reputation as an organisation

- Helping to attract and retain our best people

- Reducing recruitment costs through retention

- Avoiding any legal or compensation costs from employee grievances or equal pay claims

The gender pay gap (GPG)

One of the main frustrations for HR professionals over the years has been the confusion between equal pay and the GPG, particularly when this is reported in the media. The definition of equal pay and the GPG is different; the GPG is a measure of the average and median difference between men's and women's average earnings across an organisation or a labour market. It does not consider whether roles are carrying out similar work or require similar skills and competencies.

The GPG exists for many reasons, including:

- Women being overrepresented in low-paying roles, such as customer-service assistants and carers, and under-represented in high-paying sectors, such as investment banking and finance.

- A difference in experience due to women taking time off or reducing their hours to care for children. Working part-time can have a negative impact on pay progression.

- Lack of part-time and flexible working opportunities, especially at senior levels.

- Lack of senior female role models and mentors, which serves to discourage women from pursuing higher-paying careers.

GPG calculations

Currently in the UK, organisations with over 250 employees are required to publish their GPG.

Organisations are required to publish six numbers:

1. Mean GPG – the difference between the mean hourly rate of pay for male and female full pay relevant employees, expressed as a percentage of the hourly pay of male full pay relevant employees.

2. Median GPG – the difference between the median hourly rate of pay for male and female full pay relevant employees, expressed as a percentage of the hourly pay of male full pay relevant employees.

3. Mean bonus gap – the difference between the mean bonus amount paid to male and female employees during the twelve months prior to the snapshot date, expressed as a percentage of the bonus paid to male employees.

4. Median bonus gap – the difference between the median bonus paid to male and female employees during the twelve months prior to the snapshot date, expressed as a percentage of the bonus paid to male employees.

5. Bonus proportion – the proportion of male employees who received a bonus over the twelve months, expressed as a percentage of male employees, compared to the female employees who received a bonus in the twelve months, expressed as a percentage of the female employees.

6. Quartile pay bands – employees are organised into evenly
sized quartiles based on the ranking of all full pay relevant
employees, from highest to lowest by hourly rate of pay.

The mean or average is found by adding all numbers and then
dividing by the number of values. The median is the middle value
when a data set is ordered from least to greatest.

Whereas equal pay is purely a pay concern, the GPG is a much
wider issue. To bridge the gap, we need to understand why it exists
and not just confuse it with equal pay.

Equal pay is a legal obligation

Equal pay means that men and women
in the same employment must receive
equal pay for equal work, as laid out in
the Equality Act 2010.

The gender pay gap is a measure

The gender pay gap is a measure of the
difference between men and women's
average earnings across an
organisation or the labour force.

Publishing the six numbers that are mandatory for organisations
with over 250 employees is not good enough. In fact, these
average and median numbers don't really tell us anything about
pay; organisations should also be required to publish a narrative
report alongside their numbers explaining how the pay gap was
calculated, the reasons for the pay gap and the steps they are taking
to bridge the gap.

Closing the gap

To understand the reasons for the GPG, each organisation needs to analyse its own GPG and figure out why it exists. Here are some of the common strategies you and your organisation can use to bridge the gap.

Commit to complete flexible working. If the COVID-19 pandemic taught us anything, it is that the vast majority of people are capable of working flexibly and, in many cases, remotely. In fact, research has shown that productivity increased when people had more flexibility and autonomy and were working remotely during the pandemic.[35]

It is common for women to reduce their working hours to manage family commitments. If we allow people to work flexibly, parents – usually, but not always, women – could continue to work full-time. Flexible working isn't just allowing people to work from 8am to 4pm instead of 9am to 5pm; it is about trusting them to manage their own time as long as they are delivering their objectives.

Flexible working allows people caring for children to continue earning a high salary and enables them to have a better chance of being promoted. Having looked at data for hundreds of companies, I have seen a clear trend of many people working part-time in entry-level or less experienced roles, but as they move into senior management roles, they are expected to be available throughout the week.

Make promotions fair and transparent. If you were the captain of the school football team and had to decide between two

---

35   Goasduff, L, 'Digital Workers Say Flexibility Is Key to Their Productivity', Gartner (9 June 2021), www.gartner.com/smarterwithgartner/digital-workers-say-flexibility-is-key-to-their-productivity, accessed 30 June 2022

people of similar skill, who would you pick for the next match? You would likely pick the person you know better. It makes sense and it's human nature. We would all probably do the same thing.

The work environment isn't much different. If a manager has to choose between two people with similar skills and performance, who are they going to pick? A few groups lose out as a result, which can be linked to the pay gap:

- Parents (usually women) who may not network or socialise after work due to family commitments.

- Several ethnic minority groups don't drink alcohol and hence may choose not to network or socialise, which means they go unnoticed.

- Introverts who prefer to keep to themselves and don't network or socialise. They may quietly get on with their work and contributions, but go unnoticed.

Extroverts in the workplace: gain energy from social interaction

Introverts in the workplace: gain energy from spending time alone

Leaders should allow people to make their own choices

Make informed decisions with a career and pay framework. A career framework based on your job evaluation process allows you to make informed decisions when promoting people and giving them pay rises. It allows you to make fair and consistent decisions across your organisation. The framework will also allow you to carry out regular checks to ensure that there are no equal pay risks or unfair practices.

Stop basing salary decisions for new hires on their current salaries. We discussed this in an earlier chapter, but it can't be emphasised enough: if you want fair pay in your organisation, then you need to have a clear process and rationale for making pay decisions and not transfer inequalities from one organisation to another.

Start as you mean to go on

The easiest time to address pay inequalities is when you are hiring or promoting someone into a new role. Put a process in place so that your leaders and HR team don't lose this opportunity or become influenced by current salaries. Otherwise, when it comes to the annual pay review process, you are likely to worry about how you will find the budget to address these pay inequalities.

Alongside the GPG, we need to focus on the ethnicity pay gap, but we can't look at average numbers without a narrative. This simplifies a complex issue and doesn't explain why the gap exists or whether it is justified. This type of binary thinking and polarised argument fuels tribalism on social media and in wider discussions, which stops us from having a real, meaningful debate.

For example, if we see an ethnicity pay gap of 15%, it means the average pay of ethnic minorities is much lower than white employees. This feels wrong and it seems like the right thing to do would be to have no ethnicity pay gap, ie 0%, but this is framing a complex issue into binary thinking.

Perhaps some of the reason for the ethnicity pay gap is that many ethnic minorities for cultural reasons choose to work in careers that give them better work/life balance and more time with family. Perhaps these careers don't require years of studying for exams, learning highly technical skills or the stress of working late nights. Perhaps they are quite happy earning a lower salary for what they feel is a better quality of life.

In this scenario, simply saying that we need the ethnicity pay gap to be zero would require either:

- Paying the same salary in all roles regardless of skills or knowledge, which would be unfair to the people who choose to spend thousands of pounds on training, exams and hard work to gain extra knowledge and skills

- Forcing people from ethnic minorities to study for these qualifications and go into these careers for more money, even if it's a choice they would rather not make

I'm sure we can agree that paying an architect the same salary as a data entry worker would not be fair. It is also not fair to force ethnic minorities to make decisions about their life and career simply to suit what we perceive to be 'right' and to achieve an ethnicity pay gap of 0%. Even if we say we'll 'encourage' ethnic minorities to make certain career choices, it sounds a little arrogant.

People are different. They all contribute in different ways and value different things. I don't want to be forced or influenced into making career choices to fit in with a perceived narrative or outcome. We need equality of opportunity and equality of information, allowing everyone to make their own informed choices.

Having said that, there is so much we need to do to reduce gender and ethnicity pay gaps without forcing people to make choices that are not right for them. We can allow people to work flexibly so they can continue to progress their career and not have to decide between that and family time. Create an environment where leaders are not consciously or unconsciously promoting their friends or people who are good at networking. Have a career and pay framework that enables us to be fair and consistent. Finally, we can make sure we're not influenced by current salaries so we're paying people according to what they're worth and the contribution they make to our organisation.

There will always be some differences in pay. People are not machines and they all contribute in different ways with their unique skills and attributes.

As well as ensuring that pay is fair internally, we have to ensure it is fair externally. Otherwise, we risk losing our best people who can go elsewhere to get the right salary. How we determine whether someone is paid a fair salary externally is through a comprehensive salary benchmarking process. This doesn't mean simply going online to Google salaries for a job title. It involves a more robust process, which we covered in Chapter 5.

Having fair pay is not just about ensuring that base salaries are fair. We also need to look at bonuses and incentives. This is what we will be covering in the next chapter.

9

Variable Pay

I'm not sure if *Trading Places* is classed as a Christmas film, although you do often see it on TV around Christmas – and it does contain a drunken Santa at a company Christmas party.[36] It revolves around brothers Mortimer and Randolph Duke, owners of a trading company, arguing whether nature or nurture is the determining factor in someone's life. They bet that if they give Billy Ray Valentine, a beggar played by Eddie Murphy, all the luxuries belonging to Louis Winthorpe III, the managing director played by Dan Aykroyd, their behaviours and attitudes will reverse. It's a classic *Prince and the Pauper* tale.

Amid the hilarity are uncomfortable reminders of the extreme inequality and social/racial divides that exist on our doorsteps, and how quickly fortunes can change. Sadly, the vast divide between rich and poor has only become more relevant since the 1980s when *Trading Places* was released.

In one scene, Mortimer and Randolph are reading when the butler, Ezra, enters the room carrying two glasses of milk. At this moment, Randolph remembers Ezra's Christmas bonus and hands him a measly five dollars. Ezra sarcastically suggests that he will use the money to go to the movies – alone.

---

36   Landis, J, *Trading Places* (Paramount, 1983)

'Half of it is from me,' Mortimer reminds him, as Ezra swears under his breath and walks away.

Not all bonuses are motivating. If no thought or care goes into a bonus payment, it can do more harm than good. Let's take a look at how we should approach these payments.

What is variable pay?

The simplest definition of variable pay is pay for results, ie it is not guaranteed. These payments may be based on individual, team or organisational results. They may be financial, operational or even behavioural.

The best variable pay solutions need to emphasise two things:

- Specific goals and measures
- Simplicity and transparency

Let's have a closer look at each one.

Specific goals and measures

If the definition of variable pay is pay for results, then people need to understand how their role impacts those results. If you are looking at individual results, then what goals and measures determine personal performance? If it is at a team or organisational level, what are the specific financial, operational or strategic outcomes that will result in payment?

When you're looking at targets, it is useful to review them on a regular basis. You don't need to use a formulaic approach or punish people for missing targets, but regular reviews do help your people plan and improve their productivity.

For example, if you were training for a 10K run, would you run as fast as you can every time, or would you measure the time so you can set yourself a target and improve? What if you're not feeling well or have a slight injury? Would you adapt your target to the circumstances, understanding that the original target has become unhelpful and unrealistic? Much the same principle applies to employee and business targets.

Simplicity and transparency

You can have the best-designed reward frameworks, but if there is no transparency and employees are not aware of how they work, they are most likely going to be ineffective.

The objective of variable pay is typically to drive performance or behaviours. For this to work, people must have a sound understanding of the variable pay plans. It is also important to be simple and transparent so you can communicate clearly and set employee expectations. Otherwise, people will see variable pay as an additional element of their reward package and come to expect it every year. If they don't receive it one year, they will be disheartened and wonder why.

Variable cash pay has to be significant enough to be meaningful. Think about it from the employee's perspective and work out what they would be getting after tax. If it's a small amount, you may want to give employees a personalised gift rather than a cash bonus. The last thing you want is to provide an employee with a bonus amount so small that instead of motivating them, it leads them to swear under their breath.

Different types of bonuses

In many organisations, people tend to refer to all variable pay as a bonus, but there are subtle differences that are important to understand. To design and communicate a variable pay scheme, we need to be clear about our purpose for having it in the first place.

Bonus

Bonuses are paid to recognise a single or combination of outcomes. Typically, they are based on a mixture of individual employee performance and organisational performance. Organisations have bonuses to:

- Encourage behaviours or actions that will contribute towards the success of the organisation. They link this success to the individuals who contributed towards it.

- Make their reward package more competitive. If other organisations pay a bonus, you may feel the need to pay one as well to compete for people in the job market. For example, it may not be affordable to pay a salary of £100K, so instead you pay £80K plus an additional £20K at the end of the year if the company does well.

An annual bonus is usually communicated to all employees who are eligible and paid at the end of the financial year. Affordability tends to be based on a profit measure such as EBITDA (Earnings Before Interest, Taxes, Depreciation and Amortisation), but can also include other financial and non-financial measures. Company performance usually determines the overall bonus pot, which is then distributed among employees based on their job level and individual or team performance.

Some leaders think an annual bonus will help them retain their people and drive engagement, but this is not usually the case. No one wakes up every day feeling motivated because they're thinking about the bonus they may get in ten months. If an employee is unhappy in their job, it is unlikely that the prospect of a bonus will help you to retain them. At best, they may be willing to delay their resignation by two to three months and resign as soon as the bonus is paid into their account. Mistaking bonuses for a retention tool can be a big mistake.

An unlikely scenario

Many people come to expect their annual bonus, even though it is usually discretionary, not contractual. If you haven't communicated bonus metrics and updated people about company performance, suddenly finding out that they won't receive a bonus at the end of the year can be demotivating. Clear communication is critical when it comes to bonuses.

Profit sharing

This is an arrangement where an organisation shares a portion of its profits with employees. The difference between a profit share and a bonus is that a profit share is only paid if the organisation makes a profit. It is usually shared equally between employees, ie not based on individual performance.

An organisation may accrue some bonus payments in its budget, which means even if it were to make a net loss, it would still pay out the bonus. A profit share is not usually hierarchical like a bonus – the message is that all employees are in this together.

There may be some eligibility requirements for profit-sharing plans, for example, an employee having worked at the company for a certain period of time, but in my opinion, eligibility should begin from day one. We need to put thought and effort into the recruitment process, but once someone joins the organisation, they are part of the team just like anyone else. It's not a great message to a new hire if we say, 'Prove yourself to us, and then we may consider you to be part of the team.'

Sign-on bonus

This is a one-off bonus paid to an employee we recruit into our organisation. It's a way to make our job offer more attractive and encourage the candidate to join.

A sign-on bonus is usually paid to more senior candidates who we want to persuade to join our organisation. They may be eligible for a significant bonus in their present role, or they may have shares/ equity and resigning will mean giving these up. A sign-on bonus compensates for these losses.

Sign-on bonuses have become quite common in recent years. I am not aware of any research that suggests whether people who receive sign-on bonuses are more or less likely to stay with an organisation. My guess, based on anecdotal evidence and twenty years of reward experience, is that they are less likely. If people are attracted to your organisation because you offer a sign-on bonus, chances are they will be attracted elsewhere in a year or two by another one.

Recognition bonus

A recognition bonus is given to employees who go above and beyond to demonstrate results or behaviours that are aligned with your organisational values. This may be working hard on the delivery of a project or delivering outstanding customer service to a client.

Recognition bonuses are discretionary and unexpected. The bonus is the outcome, not the driver for the effort or behaviours. If people put in extra effort because they expect a bonus at the end of it, then it is no longer a recognition bonus but a project bonus, which must be clearly defined and communicated. Otherwise, a £100 bonus after months of hard work can end up being *demotivating*.

Recognition bonuses shouldn't be handed out willy-nilly – we need to put some thought into it. An extra £50 transferred into an employee's account (depleted after tax) will mean much less than £50 of vouchers for their favourite shop or brand. Recognition bonuses also need to be timely to encourage the same behaviours. Recognising someone six months after they delivered outstanding customer service with a client is just a nice gesture – it won't reinforce or communicate why the person is being recognised.

Retention bonus

As the name suggests, retention bonuses are used by organisations to retain their people. They are based on the premise that if someone stays with the organisation for a certain period of time, eg two to three years, they will receive an annual retention bonus. If they leave before the end of the term, they will lose out. The retention bonus has to be significant enough to induce someone to stay with the organisation.

This is the most misused and misunderstood type of bonus. Let's say you are on a three-year retention bonus. Every year, you will receive £10,000 if you stay with the company. Even if we assume that the retention bonus helps to retain you, what will you do after three years? Your total reward package has now gone down, so you'll probably either want to be put on another retention plan or seek opportunities elsewhere.

There are exceptions, of course. For example, if you want to retain someone for the delivery of a key project or if the business is closing down and it is essential to retain key roles for this closure. A retention bonus can also be a way for managers to offer a higher reward package to someone in their team if:

- This is not possible through the salary increase budget

- A significant salary increase would cause internal equity concerns

The downside of this is that it tends to result in people who are better or more aggressive at negotiating pay ending up on a retention plan. If you have retention plans in your organisation, I suggest running a quick analysis by gender. My experience with different organisations is that the vast majority of people on retention plans tend to be male.

Remember, we are talking about bonuses here and not sales incentives, which are based on specific, quantifiable outputs. Can bonuses be motivating and drive performance? Yes, to some extent, but if they are not well-defined or they are miscommunicated, they can be highly demotivating.

Like base salary, bonuses help to attract candidates and make the reward package competitive, so they need to form part of a wider reward strategy where non-financial elements are more important. For most people, their primary objectives and motivations are much more meaningful than money, like having career progression or a positive work culture.

Sales incentives

In the film *As Good as It Gets*,[37] Melvin Udall – an eccentric and offensive but successful novelist played by Jack Nicholson – suffers from obsessive compulsive disorder. That's his excuse for keeping people at a distance and for his racist, homophobic and misogynistic behaviour. He's the sort of person who would be an HR nightmare, leading several employees to file grievances.

One of his daily rituals is to have breakfast in the same café and be waited on by the same waitress: Carol, played by Helen Hunt. Melvin is constantly embarrassing himself by his lack of social skills and Carol is the only one who tolerates Melvin's behaviour (most of the time) and keeps him sane. This film is not always politically correct, but is an absolute classic that won Jack Nicholson an Oscar.

It takes his neighbour's little dog to open Melvin's heart and inspire generosity. When his neighbour Simon, played by Greg Kinnear,

---

37   Brooks, JL, *As Good as It Gets* (TriStar Pictures, 1997)

gets severely beaten and is down on his luck, Melvin decides to take them in. Finally, he's ready for his biggest challenge – expressing his love for Carol. Melvin can't bring himself to do this and he's given a pep talk by Simon, who tells him that the best thing he has going for him is his willingness to humiliate himself.

This line always reminds me of good salespeople – I mean that as a compliment. I often wonder how people can enjoy sales roles: learning their pitch, establishing contact with each lead, giving it their best shot, but frequently being ignored or rebuffed.

It's an emotional rollercoaster, up and down, that never seems to stop. Salespeople could be faced with rejection after rejection. When they lose a deal, everybody knows about it, but good salespeople just brush it off and continue to the next person or deal. I guess the best thing they've got going for them is their willingness to humiliate themselves and you've got to admire that attitude.

What are sales incentives?

Devised specifically for sales and revenue-generating teams, sales incentives or commission plans are designed to drive certain types of desirable behaviours. They are different from bonuses in a few ways:

- They usually have a much greater focus on individual performance

- They tend to be more formulaic, with specific targets and measures, compared to a discretionary bonus plan

- They are often higher payments than bonuses as sales roles typically have higher variable pay linked to revenue or profit generated by the employee, team or organisation

The design of a sales incentive is crucial, as the wrong incentive plan can lead to the wrong behaviours. Incentive programmes can be monetary or non-monetary.

Sales incentives are usually given to roles that are directly responsible for generating revenue for the company, because the objective of any sales incentive plan is to create an environment where employees want to contribute to the company's success. We ensure this by driving the right behaviours.

One of the primary objectives of sales incentive schemes in recent years has been to drive excellent customer service. If you encourage your sales teams to behave in the right way, you will achieve this goal. In turn, you will have more loyal customers who are likely to give you repeat business and recommend you to others.

The key is to make sure that your sales incentive programmes are simple and attainable, and set up in a way that's easy for everybody to understand, but there are several factors to consider. Not all salespeople are motivated in the same way.

Sales compensation challenges

The trouble with sales incentive plans is that they are often designed and managed by the sales teams themselves, rather than by HR or a sales incentive specialist. This means that each team has its own unique plan, with no consistency across the organisation, making it difficult for HR and finance to have any control or governance over the management of these plans.

Members of the sales team are usually immersed in the details and this can lead to plans getting overcomplicated. They end up measuring a variety of factors, such as number of phone calls made, time spent on the phone or number of leads generated. I worked

A CASE OF THE MONDAYS

with a client once where the sales managers were incentivising the team against measures including whether they completed their forms correctly and ticked all the boxes. The more measures a plan tracks, the harder it is to keep tabs on who is getting what commission and why. A lot of incentive programmes fail due to complexity in their recording and reporting systems.

If you're looking to hire someone and they ask about commission, your sales incentives should be easy to explain.

It all comes back to behaviour. Delivering pay-outs too quickly, for example, can drive transactional behaviours that lead to pushy sales tactics, instead of people taking the time to build meaningful relationships with customers. On the other hand, some roles are transactional so do require more regular payments. There is a balance we need to find.

How do we simplify a sales incentive plan so it's easy to understand, communicate and implement? First, we look at the objectives: what is the company trying to achieve? What behaviours are we looking to drive? Is it revenue, profit or customer service?

Designing an effective plan means:

- Assessing the performance measures that each person can directly impact

- Clearly communicating the company's strategic objectives and each employee's role

- Looking at non-monetary rewards such as coaching, training, career progression and performance management

The what and the how

We've talked about this in earlier chapters and sales incentives are no different. If anything, it's even more important that we observe *how* people perform their role when looking at sales teams. After all, salespeople have direct interactions with our existing and potential customers.

Incentive plans that focus on revenue at any cost could encourage salespeople to sell at any cost – even that all-important long-term customer relationship. Fostering customer loyalty is vital to your business: it costs five times as much to attract a new customer than to keep an existing one. When you're designing a sales incentive plan, don't just focus on the numbers, which are important, but understand what will help your people build long-term relationships and grow the business. Encourage your sales teams to behave in the right way and you will create a culture that values customer service, meaning higher customer retention and more revenue long term.

Whether a bonus or a sales incentive scheme, or a mix of the two, is the right choice across our organisations, it is essential that we continue to communicate this clearly to our people so we can manage their expectations and promote the right behaviours. What we can't manage, though, is performance. Why?

That's what we will look at in the next chapter.

10

Performance Can't Be Managed

On the surface, *Friday Night Lights* shouldn't appeal to a wide audience who don't know much about American football, let alone high-school football, but it is one of the best American dramas of recent years.[38] American football is merely the medium that allows the show to explore adversity, diversity and class, but more importantly, the series is about optimism and the triumph of the human spirit. It shows us that life isn't perfect, but it's the little things in life that are worth celebrating and that even the smallest dreams are worth chasing.

The show also features possibly the greatest television couple of all time: Coach Eric Taylor and Principal Tami Taylor. They are both inspiring in their own ways – one mentoring students in school, and the other on the field.

Anyone who watches team sports knows that the manager is often under immense pressure. The pressure of ensuring their team performs every time they get on the field. The pressure to deliver results. Coach Taylor is no different. He needs to get the most out of his players. He needs them to perform to the best of

---

38   Katims, J, *Friday Night Lights*, Season 05 Episode 30 (2010)

their ability. In the final season, Coach Taylor gives some advice to his quarterback Vince, telling him that it's not about *being* better than everyone else, it's about *striving* to be better – and that's what character is.

Coach Taylor realises that performance isn't something he can manage. All he can do is inspire his team, empower them and give them the courage to try their best. To always strive to be better. Coach Taylor isn't managing the performance of his players; he is creating an environment where they feel safe and inspired, enabling them to achieve excellence.

The system is broken

The Chartered Institute of Personnel and Development (CIPD) factsheet describes performance management as 'the attempt to maximise this value creation [the value delivered by people working in an enterprise] and ensure that employees contribute to business objectives'.[39] There's no standard definition, it explains, but performance management usually describes three activities:

- Establishing objectives through which individuals and teams can see their part in the organisation's strategy and mission

- Improving the performance of individuals and teams

- Holding people to account by linking reward and career progression

When they're discussing performance management, many people immediately think about the annual appraisal, since this is

---

39   'Performance management: an introduction', CIPD (2 December 2020), www.cipd.co.uk/knowledge/fundamentals/people/performance/factsheet#6292, accessed May 2022

traditionally how most organisations approached this topic. They think about the one or two performance conversations they have each year when their manager assesses their performance over the last twelve months and gives a performance rating. And, of course, this isn't just a performance conversation. Performance is often linked to pay, so there are much wider implications.

When employees hear about their performance rating at the end of the year, they're often confused because it's not what they expected, and it seems unfair. Where's the evidence? Even if it's not unfair, there's no time to make adjustments because it's the end of the year – and yet this will impact their pay.

This process also allows managers to say that they wanted to give another rating – but HR said no. The employee now resents HR as well as the manager, who wasn't strong enough to make a case for them.

Performance management has evolved and continues to evolve. Leaders realised that simply having one performance management conversation a year, or even two (with a mid-year review), wasn't enough.

As a result, performance management evolved into a continuous cycle, not just one-off meetings. In theory, anyway. In reality, many organisations struggled to get their managers to have regular one-to-ones with their team.

'We speak to our team all the time,' the managers would say. 'We sit next to each other. We don't need to have a one-to-one just because HR has asked us to have one. It's not adding any value for us.' Even where managers were having more regular conversations with their team, this just wasn't working. Performance management was broken and something needed to change.

Regular one-to-ones or not, managers had to meet with their team members at the end of the year and give them a performance rating. There are different types of rating systems that organisations would operate, for example, a four-point scale:

- Rating 1 = Underperformance

- Rating 2 = Average

- Rating 3 = Good

- Rating 4 = Outstanding

Managers had to place their employees based on their performance for the year, but many struggled with this and understandably so. To make matters worse, managers were given a fixed allocation of ratings they could use. If they had ten people in their team, for example, they could only rate one person outstanding, three people good, five people average and one person had to be underperforming. Regardless of whether the overall team was performing poorly or exceptionally, these were the ratings and people had to fit into this allocated distribution. This is referred to as forced distribution of performance ratings.

The problem with forced distribution

Forcing people along 'normal' distribution curves is one of the biggest challenges we have been facing as HR professionals. General Electric was famous for ranking its employees on a normal distribution curve.[40] Every year, managers had to rank 20% of their people as 'outstanding', 70% as 'high performers' and 10% as 'in need of improvement', but instead of receiving feedback,

---

40   Bates, S, 'Forced Ranking', SHRM (1 June 2003),
www.shrm.org/hr-today/news/hr-magazine/pages/0603bates.aspx, accessed May 2022

to improve their performance and support for their development, these last 10% were fired.

There are many issues here. This model assumes that bad performance is purely the fault of the employee, but there are many factors that can contribute to this, such as the working environment or their relationship with the manager. How often do we see sporting teams that perform badly, but as soon as there is a change in management, a transformation takes place in the performance?

Forcing our people into ratings is not helpful for anyone. If our recruitment team is doing an exceptional job and bringing in great talent, then isn't it possible that we may not have a 'normal' distribution?

Imagine a five-a-side football team that consists of Ronaldo, Messi, Neymar, Benzema and De Bruyne. They play a match and each player scores three goals. Who would you place in the 'needs improvement' category? With this team of superstars, no doubt that person would be offended and decide to leave, and chances are you would have to replace them with someone who is not as good.

It is widely understood now that for organisations to be successful, they need collaboration in the workplace. Collaboration enables employees to share knowledge and work more efficiently and effectively. By creating a normal distribution (whether forced or through calibration), we are effectively creating an environment where colleagues are competing with each other.

In the five-a-side football team example, if the players know they will be rated based on the number of goals scored, it's likely they will become selfish and try to score every time instead of passing the ball, even when their teammate is in a much better position.

Again, this leads to the overall team being worse off.

A conveyor belt of employees coming in and being exited out based on performance ratings leads to constant and unnecessary recruitment and redundancy costs. From an HR perspective, forcing people into a normal distribution curve gives managers an easy way out of any meaningful or difficult conversations with their teams. How many times have we heard about a leader telling someone in their team that they wanted to give them a higher rating, but HR told them this wasn't possible?

The evolution of performance management

Although General Electric finally got rid of ratings a few years ago after three decades of using this awful system, many organisations persisted with this framework. Despite this, the evolution of performance management continued as more and more organisations realised that forced distribution made absolutely no sense and scrapped it.

Instead, they would have 'calibration' meetings with managers across the business, spending hundreds of hours every year discussing the performance ratings of people. The purpose of the calibration was for managers and leaders to challenge each other and make sure there was consistency in the decision-making process.

This sounds like a good approach, but the premise behind the calibration meetings was that managers were allowed to give the ratings they wanted as long as they broadly followed a normal distribution curve, and overall as an organisation, employees should certainly be sitting along this curve. Although this process looked good in theory, allowing a little bit of leeway to managers, it was still ultimately forcing employees along a distribution curve.

The performance management evolution didn't end here. Realising that the ratings system, even with calibration, wasn't working, some organisations got rid of performance ratings altogether. This began with public announcements by organisations such as Deloitte and Accenture, then many others followed.

In some cases, it seemed more like a PR exercise and the forced distribution of performance ratings had simply been replaced with a forced distribution of another rating such as development or potential. In most cases, though, the annual appraisal and ratings were replaced with a more fluid process involving regular check-ins and feedback to measure and evaluate performance.

Why has the approach and the performance management process changed so many times over the years? We tried something, it didn't work and so we decided to come up with a new process. After a few years, the new process wasn't working that well either, so we decided to change it again.

If Schools Managed Performance Like Workplaces

How we manage performance has continued to evolve but, as usual, we should be starting with *why*. Why are we doing this? If your child is struggling in class, would you work with them to understand the support they need and give them the tools and encouragement to excel, or would you just put them on a performance improvement plan and start thinking about a replacement?

Coach Taylor knew that performance is not something we can manage. Our people can't always be better than everyone else, but we've all got to try to be better versions of ourselves. That's what character is. It's in the trying.

Enabling Excellence – redefining performance management

If you were to ask employees, including people managers, what they think when they hear the term 'performance management', they would probably respond with appraisals and evaluations, but another common response is 'performance management is about managing underperformance'. After all, if someone is an exceptional performer and an overachiever, why do you need to 'manage' their performance?

For this reason, at 3R Strategy, we don't use the term 'performance management'. Even if you do have underperformers, this will likely be a very small proportion of your employees. The vast majority of your employees, you would hope, are performing well or exceptionally well in your organisation.

Since performance is not something we can manage, we have to create an environment where people are always striving to be better. Enabling Excellence refers to a set of values that help us inspire our colleagues to be motivated and committed by building a culture of collaboration and trust. It is about looking after the people in our organisations at all levels by engaging them in our core values and supporting their development, all of which ultimately contributes to the overall success of the organisation.

There are many organisations that have a great culture and a good approach to what they call 'performance management', but they need to redefine their why. We can't just tell employees to perform. What we can do is provide the right conditions and culture to promote health, wellbeing and productive relationships, so our colleagues can flourish in our organisations.

To establish trust in the performance management process, we must completely rethink our approach. We have to change our language, our process and our culture. The language we use is important and we need to shift to using more positive language, and a name that doesn't imply that we can control and manage the performance of our employees. A move away is needed from annual or bi-annual appraisal and performance conversations at set times during the year, to a process that is much more flexible and results in ongoing feedback and dialogue. And, we must move away from a culture of competition to one of collaboration and trust.

Enabling Excellence is not an HR process, but the role of a manager. For it to be successful, building trust with their team should be one of the deliverable objectives of each manager.

Simply replacing one process with another won't make much difference. Often, organisations spend millions to change a five-point rating system to a three-point rating system, but what we really need is a change in culture, as well as training for managers and understanding from them that people management is the most important aspect of their role. It's not something they need to get out of the way to do their real job; this is their job.

There are two aspects of Enabling Excellence. The first is about moving away from a culture of competition to a culture of collaboration and trust. Whether or not you choose to use performance ratings, we need to move to a flexible process with regular and sometimes difficult, but necessary, conversations.

As part of this process, people would agree their objectives, and these can be updated regularly with their manager. It's about sharing these objectives and our achievements with the wider team every quarter, providing more frequent and meaningful forums for updates and to exchange feedback.

Research shows that you can measure the health of a relationship, health of a team or even an organisation by the average lag time between identifying and discussing problems.[41] This means that the health of our teams and organisations is being impacted by these important conversations, which are either not taking place, taking place too late or not taking place well.

So how do we enable these conversations to take place? When we have a culture of collaboration and trust it becomes easier to hold deeper, more honest conversations that transform our relationships in the workplace. By being prepared to hold these conversations, instead of avoiding them, we also ensure clarity over responsibilities and expectations. This enables us to achieve excellence.

But we don't just want colleagues to be able to have these conversations. We want these conversations to be successful. Research shows that the most important factor in predicting the success of these conversations is creating psychological safety right from the start.

---

41   Grenny, J, 'Writing the Third Edition of Crucial Conversations: Behind the Scenes', Crucial Skills (10 November 2021), https://cruciallearning.com/blog/writing-the-third-edition-of-crucial-conversations-behind-the-scenes, accessed 4 July 2022

Psychological safety allows us to share ideas, questions and concerns leading to productive conversations and ongoing feedback where everyone is working towards a common goal.

When psychological safety is low, colleagues hold back in meetings and 1-2-1s, which results in diminished conversation. Diversity of thought is reduced, and new ideas are missed, and our opportunities for improvement are not challenged.

The second part of Enabling Excellence goes back to the fact that performance isn't something we can manage, but it is impacted by many factors. How are we measuring these factors and using this data to support our colleagues?

We do this through a comprehensive excellence survey which looks at the factors that impact performance. Our colleagues need:

- great physical health; nutrition, inactivity, sleep, and fatigue can all play a significant role

- balanced psychological and mental health

- support around factors outside of work which affect them at work

- a strong personal work ethic

- satisfaction with the job that they do

- engagement with their team

- commitment to the organisation – our vision and values

- good relationship with their manager

- a corporate culture that makes it possible for them to achieve excellence

- the right working environment: whether they're working from home or in the office

It's the collective wellbeing of employees that leads to the wellbeing and success of the organisation. This is what we need to strive for.

There is so much more that can be said about performance management, but that's for another book. That said, many organisations want to pay for performance, so it's important to understand that before we link performance to pay, we have to be sure that our Enabling Excellence process is working and trusted by our colleagues. This brings us neatly on to the next chapter, in which we will look more closely at paying for performance.

11

Pay For Performance

There has been a lot written in recent years about pay for performance such as the New York Times bestseller *Drive* by Daniel Pink.[42] In this book, Pink talks about extrinsic and intrinsic motivation and makes a compelling case that incentives just don't work most of the time.

There are two types of work, he explains: algorithmic and heuristic. An algorithmic task is where you follow a set of instructions down a defined path that leads to a single conclusion. An heuristic task has no instructions or defined path and could be creative or analytical.

A lot of his research refers to the 'if, then' incentives. *If* individuals deliver a specific task, *then* they will receive a reward. He explains that these incentives can increase motivation in the short run, but reduce it in the long run because they lack any intrinsic motivation. Furthermore, they work for algorithmic tasks, but not for heuristic tasks that require complex analytical thinking. In fact, they can even lead to worse performance.

There are many examples in Pink's book, including one of sales quotas that led to undesired behaviours, where 'if, then' incentives caused people to make decisions they may not have ordinarily

---

42   Pink, DH, Drive: *The surprising truth about what motivates us* (Riverhead Hardcover, 2009)

made with a narrow focus on the finish line. Does this mean that there is no place for incentives in pay and reward? I have been in workshops with senior management teams that have quoted Daniel Pink and explained that bonuses don't work for complex tasks. Interestingly enough, though, they themselves were on a bonus.

In Chapter 3, we talked about Atticus Finch. One of his famous quotes from *To Kill a Mockingbird* is about how you can never truly understand a person until you consider things from their point of view – 'until you climb into [their] skin and walk around in it'.[43]

This is often the problem in the corporate world, particularly in senior management teams. We can assume that certain things won't work based on how we think others will react. We can even seek research and examples to validate our thinking, but the leadership teams themselves are exceptions, of course, and remain on a bonus plan.

Where incentives go wrong

How many senior management teams in the past believed that their employees were not capable of working flexibly from home? They had to be in the office. There were a few exceptions, though: the senior management team were clearly responsible and experienced enough to manage their own time. It took the pandemic for these senior leaders to realise that not only can this work for everyone, but most people are more productive with autonomy.

We cannot make decisions about employees that are not consistent. If a senior management team feels that bonuses and incentives don't

---

43   Lee, H, *To Kill a Mockingbird* (JB Lippincott & Co, 1960)

work, then they can by all means get rid of them, but they certainly cannot put themselves on a bonus or any long-term incentives. In fact, with the high bonus payments at executive level, there is a much greater risk of undesired behaviours among senior managers focusing on achieving them, as we saw with banking bonuses and the 2008 economic crash.

Extrinsic vs. Intrinsic

There are a couple of big flaws with the arguments against incentives. For a start, they are often based on simplistic artificial experiments. Giving people a few pounds extra for completing a task is not comparable to a meaningful bonus or pay increase in the workplace which impacts people's livelihoods. The 'if, then' incentives are archaic and shouldn't be put in place in a corporate environment; the research study referenced in *Drive* rightly points out that this can lead to a narrow focus and an easy route to the finish line instead of teams working in alignment towards the big picture.

For example, asking salespeople to make X number of calls or spend X number of minutes on the phone (as some organisations do) is not a good approach at all. These tasks themselves do not guarantee a successful outcome, and by focusing on them in the work environment, we lose sight of the big picture. A bonus or an incentive needs to be thought through properly to drive the right behaviours and support our colleagues in achieving individual and our organisation's collective success. Almost all the simplified experiments are irrelevant and not comparable to work-related incentives.

We also can't look at incentives in isolation; there are many aspects of reward and recognition, and the two need to go together. If a job is not intrinsically motivating, there is no sense of purpose or belonging among the team, and team members often have a poor relationship with their manager. A bonus or incentive is not going to make any difference to this situation and may even demotivate the team members.

Perhaps your bonuses or incentives are not working or driving performance because they are perceived to be unfair as people don't trust the performance management process. Perhaps you have no transparency over who the high performers are and people believe line managers are simply paying incentives to their favourite employees. Perhaps the bonus payments for so-called 'exceptional' performance over twelve months are so small that the employees actually feel insulted instead of rewarded.

Pay for performance can work but it is not right for all organisations or roles. In some sectors, for example medical care, it would be a terrible idea. Many organisations that have pay for performance also get it completely wrong. We've talked at length about the pitfalls of the performance management process in organisations. How can we possibly pay for performance fairly, consistently and effectively when our approach to 'performance' is completely broken?

Getting pay for performance right

Maybe the problem is not that incentives don't work, but that we need to be clear about what we mean by performance and ensure that this process is fair. Regardless of the reason, though, pay for performance doesn't seem to be working for the majority of organisations.

A Willis Towers Watson survey shows that only one-third of organisations found that their base-pay initiatives were effective at paying for performance.[44] Organisations are either seeking to improve their approach or scrap pay for performance altogether.

For pay for performance to work, there are two things that need to come together. Several academic studies and research from McKinsey & Company indicate that the procedure, ie the process of how people are treated, and perception of fairness are much more important than the outcome of pay and reward.[45] An outcome may bring about short-term satisfaction, but a fair and just process will result in a change in long-term engagement and commitment. Therefore, if an organisation doesn't have a performance management process that is fair or perceived to be fair, then it doesn't really matter how it designs its incentive schemes.

Secondly, we need to start with purpose. Many people join certain organisations, for example those in the charity sector, because they identify with their sense of purpose. The objective of pay

44   Wisper, L, 'Purpose-driven pay for performance', WTW (8 February 2021), www.wtwco.com/en-GB/Insights/2019/11/purpose-driven-pay-for-performance, accessed May 2022

45   Hancock, B; Hioe, E; Schaninger, B, 'The fairness factor in performance management', McKinsey & Company (5 April 2018), www.mckinsey.com/business-functions/people-and-organizational-performance/our-insights/the-fairness-factor-in-performance-management, accessed May 2022

for performance should be to engage employees by aligning the organisation's sense of purpose with the employees' purpose and desire to help the organisation achieve that purpose.

Purpose goes beyond making the shareholders profit. Already, many large organisations are moving away from only using financial measures to much wider metrics such as ESG (Environmental, Social and Governance). This is partly driven by the fact that employees prefer to work for organisations that have a clear sense of purpose and show corporate responsibility,[46] and this preference is even stronger in Generation Z employees.

If you're planning to have a pay-for-performance culture, ask yourself if these two factors are working for you:

- Do your employees think your performance management process is fair?

- Does your organisation have a clear sense of purpose that employees identify with?

If you're unsure about either question, then maybe a pay-for-performance culture isn't the right approach for you.

Think of your bonus pot as a pie. This pie will be divided among your employees. If you give one person a bigger piece of the pie, someone else will be taking a smaller piece. Will they be able to clearly see the rationale for this decision or will they resent it because it feels completely subjective or even like favouritism? Either way, how can you build a culture of trust and collaboration when everyone is competing for a bigger slice of the pie?

---

46   Aziz, A, 'The Power Of Purpose: The Business Case For Purpose (All The Data You Were Looking For Pt 2)', *Forbes* (7 March 2020), www.forbes.com/sites/afdhelaziz/2020/03/07/the-power-of-purpose-the-business-case-for-purpose-all-the-data-you-were-looking-for-pt-2, accessed 30 June 2022

Pie for Performance

The exception to this is sales roles where the size of the pie is not fixed. If an individual performs well, this results in higher revenue or profit (ie a bigger pie), so their higher sales incentive doesn't result in someone else losing out.

If you're now questioning your pay-for-performance culture and whether you should have a bonus at all, there is an alternative. This is a profit share where everyone gets an equal slice of the pie as long as they are contributing to the wider team and organisation, which should cover the vast majority of your employees. Your exceptional performers will still be rewarded through career and pay progression since they are more likely to be capable of taking on more responsibility.

Pay is only part of the puzzle

We all like to feel valued and appreciated. A job well done deserves recognition, whether it comprises of a pat on the back or winning an award. In fact, recognising achievements is one of the best ways to improve employee engagement.

Plus, recognition works both ways. It is not only motivating for the recipient, but for the giver, too. It feels good to praise and acknowledge someone else's success.

Furthermore, recognition is free; but don't get too excited. Recognition isn't an alternative to base pay or a bonus. If instead of getting their monthly salary, an employee simply got a handwritten thank-you note from the CEO, they'd be annoyed. If they got paid their monthly salary and also received a handwritten note from their CEO thanking them for their work and contribution, that would be pretty special.

A pay strategy aligned to your reward principles, supported by a culture of recognition, is highly effective and creates a positive work culture.

Effective recognition

While giving pay rises when they're due is important, a small investment in employee recognition goes much further. For instance, if your organisation allocated 0.2% to 0.3% of its payroll to an employee recognition budget, this could have a significant impact on engagement, because when you adopt effective employee recognition programmes, you reinforce and encourage desired behaviours.

Say your 0.3% payroll budget was used to bump up someone's pay; if they're on an annual salary of £50,000, this would result in a £150 pay increase. After tax, they may see an extra £5 a month in their bank account. They may not even notice it.

Imagine instead that during the year you give that employee Amazon vouchers or a thoughtful gift within the same budget to recognise exceptional performance or behaviours that are aligned to the organisational values. This will mean so much more than the extra £5 a month in their bank account.

Knowing what recognition is and how to implement it is vital for long-term employee engagement. Fundamentally, it boils down to four key principles. Recognition should be:

- **Specific**. A general statement about how great someone is won't be helpful in the long run. It's better to praise particular actions, behaviours or how someone handled a difficult situation.

- **Timely**. This is probably the most important element. Immediate recognition will have a much greater impact than saving up remarks for an annual or bi-annual review.

- **Meaningful**. We can start with our initial intention to share a 'thank you' and expand our thoughts to make our recognition more personal and meaningful. Thank you for what? What actions or behaviours made us want to recognise them?

- **Genuine**. Genuine appreciation is about showing that you care not just about the performance and achievements of your people, but their emotional wellbeing as well.

Recognising your desired behaviours

In Part One, we talked about values and behaviours. A really effective way of reinforcing these in the workplace is through a culture of recognition that acknowledges colleagues for demonstrating them.

Some companies choose to publish employee of the month or employee of the year recognition for all to see. Others give out quarterly awards with gifts ranging in monetary value according to the level of achievement, but the vast majority of recognition is the everyday thank-yous and verbal praise for colleagues. As a key recognition principle is for it to be 'timely', we shouldn't wait for monthly and annual award ceremonies to recognise our colleagues.

Introverts vs. Extroverts

Introverts and extroverts prefer to receive recognition in different ways. While some enjoy the limelight, others dislike public displays and might prefer to be mentioned in the company newsletter or a one-to-one meeting. This is where we as leaders need to make recognition specific to the person by understanding their preferences.

We need to aim to be consistent too. Often, when there is no company-wide strategy in place, different departments will set up and manage their own recognition programmes. The problem with this fragmented approach is that it can dampen the overall impact of recognition across the organisation. If there isn't a clear recognition strategy, different parts of the organisation could be recognising people for different reasons, which can send mixed messages.

Pay is boring, but recognition is fun

Things That Have Never Happened

Has an employee ever complimented you on your pay policy? I doubt many employees even read the whole policy. They just want to get paid their salary at the end of the month and are not that concerned with how this gets done, but when something goes wrong, they make sure that the payroll people know it immediately so they can fix it.

Managing payroll is a complex task and payroll teams don't really get the credit they deserve. They are only noticed when things go wrong. We as leaders need to get into the habit of recognising any colleagues who often go unnoticed; we don't always have to wait for 'exceptional' performance.

Although pay is boring, recognition can be a lot of fun. It could be anything from saying a quick thank you after a productive meeting to applauding someone via email and copying in their manager. There's so much opportunity to experiment with different types of gifts, formal and informal recognition, and even public recognition through newsletters and award ceremonies.

It's great to have formal recognition programmes with monthly, quarterly or annual awards for achievements or behaviours. Ultimately, though, it's the spontaneous everyday conversations that will make the biggest difference.

This brings Part Two and our overview of pay, performance and recognition to a close. Now it's time for you to get 'hands on' in Part Three with some practical roadmaps to pay transparency.

PART THREE
YOUR ROADMAP TO PAY TRANSPARENCY

12

Developing Your Own Reward Strategy And Principles

In Part Two, we discussed the importance of pay transparency in building trust and driving employee engagement, but how do we set off on the journey to pay transparency? It first requires us to figure out where we are now and where we want to go.

Our approach to pay can be split up into three categories:

1. What do we pay our employees?

2. How do we make pay decisions?

3. Why do we manage pay the way we do?

If you've read Simon Sinek's book *Start With Why*, you'll be familiar with the golden circle.[47] Simon talks about the fact that we tend to go from the outside in, from the clearest thing (what) to the fuzziest thing (why), but inspired leaders and organisations, regardless of size and industry, all communicate from the inside out.

---

47   Sinek, S, *Start With Why: How great leaders inspire everyone to take action* (Portfolio, 2009)

The same is true when it comes to pay. All leaders communicate to employees *what* they will pay for a role. Fewer leaders, as the organisation grows in size, think about *how* they're making these pay decisions and whether they have put in place any policies and processes. Even fewer will know *why* they manage pay the way they do by having a clear reward strategy and principles that they communicate to employees.

Reward strategy and principles

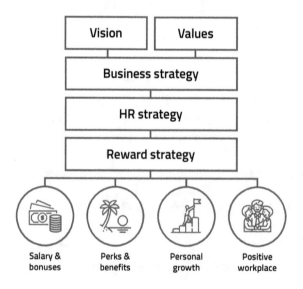

Let's start with why. The reward strategy and principles of your organisation do not sit in isolation; they are directly linked to your organisational vision and values. In the same way that your organisational values help define its culture, your reward strategy and principles define how you will approach pay and reward and enable you to clearly communicate this to your employees. To do this, you need to have a detailed look at where you are now and where you want to be.

In *Alice's Adventures in Wonderland*,[48] Alice is walking for a long time until she notices a cat perched on a tree trunk. She asks the cat which way she ought to go and the cat replies that it depends where she wants to get to. Alice tells the cat that she doesn't much care.

'Then it really doesn't much matter which way you go,' he replies.

This exchange between Alice and the Cheshire Cat applies perfectly to setting a reward strategy and your approach to specific elements of pay. Whatever you do, don't be like Alice and start planning your journey without knowing where you want to get to.

Where do you want to go?

That is the first step in setting the reward strategy and principles for your organisation. Before you go into any detail about your strategy or design of pay, ask yourself and the leaders where you're going as an organisation.

We will now go through the process 3R Strategy follows with each client. Use this process to think about your destination so you can figure out how to get there. There may be different routes you could take, but the process will give you guidance on how you can figure them out for yourself.

Finding your destination

Unlike Alice, you need to determine:

1. Where you are now. How do you currently manage pay and reward in your organisation?

---

48   Carroll, L, *Alice's Adventures in Wonderland* (Macmillan, 1865)

2. What is your destination? If you head towards your vision or business strategy in the next five to ten years, how would you like to manage pay and reward?

By understanding these two positions in relation to your approach to reward, you will be able to determine the steps you need to take to get to your desired destination. When the 3R Strategy team works with clients, we have a workshop with the leadership team to discuss this in more detail. You can facilitate this with your leadership team.

Start with a focused discussion

The way to do this is to focus the conversation by asking specific questions. A general discussion on pay tends to go off on a tangent with leaders citing personal stories or examples from their team. Instead, you want this to be a philosophical discussion.

For example, what do you currently communicate to employees about pay? What would you like to communicate to them in the future? Do you currently differentiate for performance or any other factors? Would you like to differentiate in the future or treat everyone the same from a pay perspective?

Go through this exercise as an HR team. Talking about where you want your organisation to go in this way leads to a constructive discussion that you can take to your leadership team to get their input. Their feedback ensures that when you share the details of the reward framework you subsequently develop, this won't come as a complete surprise to senior leaders, which makes it easier for you to get approval.

Once you have feedback from the business leaders, you can articulate your reward principles. These must be aligned to the values of your organisation and incorporate some of this language.

What is a reward principle?

Reward principles define your approach to pay and reward, and why you manage pay the way you do.

For example, a reward principle could be to be transparent, but you need to make sure you really are transparent in how you manage pay and reward. What does that mean in practice? Don't just have a principle, but clearly articulate what that principle (eg being transparent) means in your organisation. Think about this in relation to the pay transparency scale.

I would recommend having between three and six reward principles. With each one, challenge yourself and your organisation's HR and leadership teams and think about whether you will really do this in practice. If your leadership team does not want to publish pay ranges or communicate the company approach to career and pay progression, then 'being transparent' is probably not the right reward principle for your organisation. Your employees will see through it, no pun intended...

Once you have your reward principles set in place, always refer back to these principles. Are you considering different options for a new bonus scheme or sales incentives, for example? Test each option against your reward principles to see how relevant it is.

Your reward strategy

Once you have decided upon your reward principles, you can start thinking about how you want to approach the four pillars of workplace fulfilment in your reward strategy. As the graphic shows, these pillars are:

- Pay

- Benefits

- Positive workplace

- Personal growth

Here is a list of questions to get you thinking about your approach to reward and how you want to change or develop new policies. There are a lot of questions here and you don't necessarily have to go through all of them, but you can pick out the ones that are important for you.

- Does the current reward strategy or approach to pay and reward align with the culture of the organisation? For example, is it consistent with your values?

- What is your company's preferred position in relation to the market? For example, do you want to pay at the median or at the UQ/LQ?

- How does your organisation determine base salary? Do you use salary surveys to look at the external market? Is it based on skills and responsibilities or performance? Do you consider internal equity?

- Do you know where you typically recruit from? Are you participating in the right salary survey or is there a better source? This is covered in more detail in the next chapter.

- How do you determine pay progression? Is it linked directly to performance ratings or implicitly to performance? Is this the right approach for you? If not, what should pay progression be linked to?

- How do you link pay progression to career progression?

- Are there any roles that are difficult to recruit in your organisation? Is it pay or other factors that make it difficult for you to attract the right candidates?

- Should you have a consistent way of managing pay and reward for all roles in the organisation or are there some roles that need to be managed differently?

- Do you have a process for evaluating jobs in your organisation? If so, is this the right approach? If not, what type of job evaluation scheme should you adopt? Job evaluation is covered in more detail in Chapter 6.

- How does your organisation ensure that there are no equal-pay risks?

- Do your employees trust the performance management process?

- Is there any link between pay and organisational performance, for example, profit sharing or a bonus for all employees related to the success of the organisation?

- Are you confident that your incentives (eg bonus or sales incentives) are driving the right behaviours from your people?

- Do you feel that you are offering the right range of benefits given the changing demographics of your employees?

- Are you getting a good return on your investment in your employee benefits? When it comes to employee benefits, you need to recognise that not everyone wants the same thing. Research shows there are vast generational differences in benefit preferences as well as differences based on people's personal situations.[49]

- Who makes pay and reward decisions in your organisation? Is it the managers or is it driven centrally by HR?

What we Tend to THINK People want

What People REALLY want

Reward policies and processes

After you've established your reward principles and strategy – your why – you can also look at your policies and processes – your how.

How we manage pay can, and will, differ considerably from organisation to organisation, but all the reward policies and processes we have in place can be broken down into two steps to help us determine 'what' we pay everyone.

Step 1: Evaluate our roles. We evaluate our organisation's roles by understanding the level of skills and responsibilities required. For example, is it an entry-level or developing role, or does it require full competence and highly technical skills? By carrying

49   Sackett, H, 'The Bottom Line of Benefits for a 5 Generation Workforce', Amwins (17 August 2021), www.amwins.com/resources-insights/article/the-bottom-line-of-benefits-for-a-5-generation-workforce, accessed 30 June 2022

out this evaluation, we can determine a benchmark or salary range for the role.

Step 2: Evaluate the individual. We evaluate the individual doing each role to determine where to position them within the salary or benchmark range. For example, someone newly promoted might be positioned at the entry point of the pay range, while someone else who is fully established and perhaps even coaching others in the role may be at the higher end of the range.

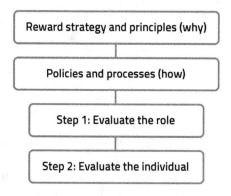

At 3R Strategy, we have devised a measurement tool so you can discover whether you have the right policies and processes in place, your current score and guidance on how you can make improvements. Before you carry on with this section of the book, why not complete our free audit and get your score? Go to yourscore.3r-strategy.com and you will receive an instant personalised report. You can then use this alongside this section of the book.

Developing a fair and transparent approach to pay is a journey, and like any journey, it needs a starting point and a destination. The online survey will give you a detailed breakdown of your starting point. What we will cover in the rest of this book will help you figure out your destination. What you don't want to do is to set off on your journey without having clarity on where you are going, like Alice in Wonderland.

13

Getting The Right Data

If you ask leaders in many organisations how they make decisions about people in their teams, the answer is often 'I use my gut feeling' along with 'I research online and look at recruitment surveys'. In other words, these managers have examined roles being advertised and the salaries other companies are offering so they have a gut feeling of what is the right amount. Occasionally, you meet the executive who thinks they know everything and has convinced themselves that it's not a gut feeling, it's a fact, but if you dig deeper, you'll generally find it's a 'fact' based on anecdotal evidence.

In most functions, organisations have a data team or at least one data specialist. Finance has always been a data function. Perhaps that's why it is considered so vital. Marketing has data and insight teams, analysing customers to understand their behaviours and predict future outcomes. IT and sales functions also manage large amounts of data.

The HR team should be making informed decisions based on research and data as well. These decisions affect people's lives. Who gets a pay rise? Who gets the new job or a promotion? It's not a science and we still have to make decisions, but they can be informed decisions.

Instead of taking on a policing role, forcing managers to accept policies and approaches, we as HR professionals can all be consultants, building relationships and influencing decisions based on compelling data. There are many ways that we can use data to improve our organisational working environment, policies and practices. In this chapter, we will focus on data from a pay and reward perspective.

External data – pick a survey to participate in

Salary surveys provide benchmark information on rates of pay that organisations can use to measure their compensation packages and benefits offering as well as HR policies and practices against the external market. Applicable to both current employees and new hires, these surveys provide the basis of internal reward frameworks and budgeting of future salaries.

The reason I say 'participate' in a survey is because pretty much all good data sources require participation to be effective. If organisations could simply pay to purchase the data, then there would be no incentive to take the time and effort to participate and add to the data. Requiring participation ensures there is a robust database as well as the integrity and accuracy of the data. When you submit your data, you will be required to think about the skills and responsibilities of your roles and assign codes based on a set of rules or a common framework.

If managers send recruitment surveys your way, thank them and accept this information as a good reference point, but explain that the data has flaws, as we discussed in Chapter 4. They are:

- Almost always based on job titles rather than the responsibilities of the role

- Based on advertised salaries, which can be a wide range and not necessarily reflective of the market, as final salaries offered to candidates can vary from the advertised range

For pay data, every survey provider has their own method of job evaluation to ensure a balanced comparison between jobs of a similar level, rather than relying on job titles. They also tend to have a robust process in place to validate submissions from organisations and get in touch to review any data that may be a potential anomaly. These survey companies use analytical tools to review large amounts of data, remove outliers and ensure that organisations with thousands of employees are not overrepresented in the survey.

While there is a cost associated with purchasing pay and reward data, and some organisations are often put off by this, it is actually one of the most cost-effective investments you can make as an HR team. Costs can range from a few hundred pounds to a few thousand pounds, so of course you want to purchase the right survey for your situation. How do you do this? Let's have a look.

Step 1 – Choosing your peer group

The first thing you need to determine when you're selecting your pay and reward survey is your comparator group. When given this challenge, many leaders tend to think about their immediate competitors. Instead, ask your leadership team, HR business partners and recruitment team which organisations and sectors you are really recruiting from.

If you work in an insurance company, for example, for the vast majority of your roles, such as HR, finance, marketing and IT, it's likely that you could be recruiting from anywhere within the financial services sector or, in fact, any sector at all. Would you only recruit an HR advisor or a finance analyst from another insurance company? Probably not.

Sure, there will be exceptions; some roles may only be recruited from the insurance sector. If so, you could treat them differently rather than basing your entire pay structure on the insurance sector because of these few roles. Define your sector as broadly as you can so you have good, robust data. Once you've defined a broad sector, or even multiple sectors, some surveys allow you to select your own unique peer group of companies from the full sample.

Next, think about where you are recruiting from geographically. Are you recruiting mainly from the local area or could people work remotely and be based anywhere in the country? This will help to identify your peer group because if you're only recruiting from the local market, then it narrows this group down.

Step 2 – Getting data for all your roles

The next step is to check that any external data you are getting will include data for the vast majority or all of your roles. If you want to find data for corporate functions (finance, HR, marketing, etc), then these will be covered in almost all salary and reward surveys. You may have some industry-specific roles or roles you think are niche, but it may be that it's the job title that is unique and the same skills exist in other sectors as well.

An exception may be where a role is managing an internal technology or process which is either unique to your organisation or becoming obsolete and therefore does not exist in the market.

In this case, you are better off coming up with a different solution to retain this person rather than trying to get relevant market data. You may look at some sort of a retention plan or even train another person in the team to mitigate the risk of dependency on one person.

You will only be able to get data for your industry-specific roles in surveys that cater to that industry. For example, you will find data for pricing and claims roles in the financial services or insurance sector surveys. If you're looking for biotechnology or medical research jobs, you will probably need to participate in a pharmaceutical sector or life sciences survey. If you're looking for data for publishing or television jobs, then you will have to participate in a media or publishing sector survey.

You may be able to get all your data from a single survey, but if you have the budget, it is certainly worth investing in getting a secondary source as well.

Step 3 – Participation process and reporting of data

Once you've decided which survey or surveys you want to participate in, the next step is to determine who will be completing the survey submission and set aside some time for them to do this. To do this job properly and help you with designing your career framework (covered later in this chapter), this person or people need to hold conversations with the business leaders or at least your HR business partners to get a better understanding of the organisational roles. Alternatively, if you have up-to-date job descriptions, they can go through these to understand and evaluate tasks and responsibilities.

Before you start the process, ask the survey provider(s) if they can run a training session with your team, particularly those people responsible for completing your survey submission. Alternatively, if you're working with reward consultants, they can provide you with some training on job evaluation and the survey submission process.

The survey data is only as good as the data being submitted by each organisation. Don't go through this process in a rush just to get access to the data. Many years ago, when I worked in a team that produced these salary surveys, we used to have a saying: 'Rubbish in, rubbish out'. If you want good data from the report, make sure you put in the time and effort to provide a good submission.

Ask the survey company to provide you with results in Excel format. You don't want to waste your time running through pages of reports and typing up salary data yourself, potentially leading to errors. Preferably, you want online access where you can run custom peer groups, select the list of companies you want to include in your sample and filter your results by elements such as location and sub-sector.

Step 4 – Data reporting and analysis

Some survey companies will give you access to data as soon as you sign up and agree to participate, while others will wait for you to submit your data, and then give you the final report. Depending on the time of the year, you may have to wait until the report is published before you are given access.

Reports are usually published using one of two methodologies:

- Company-weighted
- Incumbent-weighted

Broadly speaking, company-weighted reporting gives equal weight to every participating company. For example, if there are ten companies in the sample, each company has a 10% weighting towards the final data. Incumbent-weighted reporting gives equal weight to each employee in the sample. This means that if there are ten companies in the sample, nine of which employ a project manager and a tenth that employs five project managers, the tenth company will have a higher weighting and impact on the report. As survey companies tend to ensure that no single company completely dominates the sample, incumbent-weighted reporting is the more common approach.

There is no right or wrong approach; each has its pros and cons. If you're a data geek like me, you can ask survey companies which approach they use or if they offer both.

When you're analysing and reporting data, refer back to your reward principles and strategy. Do you want to be a market median payer or do you have another reference point? NB: 3R Strategy uses the median rather than the average because if there are anomalies – for example, a handful of really highly paid employees in one or two companies – this can distort the average, whereas it has little impact on the median if the rest of the sample is consistent.

Let's assume your reference point is the median. Still carry out your analysis against the UQ and LQ to look at the spread of the data, choose which data and information you want to include, and clearly separate your internal data from the external market data as in the table. Your compa-ratio represents the position of each employee's salary against the market. It is:

Employee salary/relevant market data salary

If an employee's salary is £90,000 and market median data is £100,000, for example, then the employee's compa-ratio is 0.90.

Internal data		Marketing data				
Employee ID	Base Salary	Job Code	25th	Median	75th	Compa ratio

After you've done your analysis, format your data and put it into a slide deck or document. This also needs to explain how you've done your analysis and what exactly you want to show your business leaders so they can make more informed decisions.

Using data to create a career framework

Where do you start to create a career framework? The good news is that you've already started. You have your reward principles and strategy. You have market data and you've participated in a salary survey which led you to evaluate your jobs against the survey company's job evaluation framework.

Now you can look at where you matched your employees to examine the spread of employees across your organisation. How many people do you have in entry-level or developing roles? How many people are experienced and fully established in their roles and careers? How many leaders do you have?

Use your data submission for the salary survey and put together a summary of your employees in different parts of the organisation. Represent this in a one-pager with a table showing your functions (HR, finance, etc) as well as levels of seniority (graduate, manager, senior manager, etc), like the table.

	HR	Finance	Marketing	Legal
Support	2			
Graduate	1		2	1
Manager			1	
Senior Manager	1	1		1

When you look at an overview of your organisation like this, it gives you a clear picture and sense of what sort of career framework would suit it.

There are many things that will help determine the type of framework that will work for your organisation, which include your reward principles and strategy. For example, if one of your reward principles is to be flexible, then having many narrow grades probably won't work for you. Have your reward principles in front of you and think about narrow and broad bands. Which approach is more in line with your organisation's principles and philosophy?

The concept of narrow and broad bands is subjective. A framework you consider to be broad may be narrow to someone else, so find out what is right for your organisation and culture. Your career framework will also help define your pay structure.

Here are some questions to ask yourself and your leadership team to help you decide on your career framework:

- Do you want flexibility where you can adjust role responsibilities without having to change the career band every time? If so, broad bands are suited to this.

- Do you want your career framework to be reflective of the external market so you can adjust pay and offer higher salaries when necessary without always putting people on a higher band? If so, broad bands are suited to this.

- Is internal equity a priority for you? Do you want to ensure there is equal pay for equal work and people are not being treated unfairly? If so, narrow bands are more suited to this, although you can still carry out an equal pay audit with broad bands.

- Do you want to have clearly defined roles and responsibilities within which people operate so that you can publish salary ranges for each role? If so, narrow bands are suited to this. You tend to see this within the public sector.

- Do you have a hierarchical culture? Is this desirable and aligned to your reward principles? If so, narrow bands lead to hierarchy, whereas broad bands allow more flexibility.

Next steps

These questions help you think about the type of career framework that would suit your organisation. Here are the next steps.

Step 1: Identify functional areas. Identify the number of broad functional areas across your organisation (HR, marketing, sales). You don't want too many or too few. As a guide, you will probably find there are between eight and fifteen.

Step 2: Define your customised career framework and number of bands/levels. Using the table we looked at earlier for your roles, the questions above and your future reward principles, determine the number of bands that would work for you.

Step 3: Develop descriptions for each band:

- **Option 1:** describe the skills and responsibilities required to be in a role at each band/level. Use bullet points and make your descriptions generic so they apply to roles across the organisation and not just in one or two business areas. A good balance between keeping the framework relatively simple while having enough detail to allow meaningful evaluations is six to eight bullet points to define each career band.

- **Option 2:** if you want to go into more detail, you can
  define a set of factors (for example problem solving or
  autonomy) and develop descriptions for each of these
  factors for your career bands. These factors describe
  the skills required at each band and how the complexity
  of those skills increases as employees move to a higher
  band. For example, will the employee be able to navigate
  through complex problems in their day-to-day tasks or
  need guidance from more experienced colleagues? This will
  become your own bespoke job evaluation process.

Step 4: Map all your employees. Use the descriptions from
Step 3 to map all your employees into your new customised career
framework. The salary survey submission you completed should
give you a great starting point for this exercise. You can look at
where you matched your roles in the survey and translate that on
to your career framework.

Step 5: Validate with your business leaders. Validate the
role mapping you carried out in Step 4 with each business area
leader. Split up your roles by business area or the broad functional
areas you looked at in Step 1, which places all the roles with similar
skills together and makes it easy to compare them. Remember to
tell the business leaders that you are placing roles in each band and
not people. Ask them to think about recruiting a new person into
the role. What skills and competencies would they be looking for?

Step 6: Develop a pay structure. Finally, you need to analyse
market data and set up a pay structure around your career
framework. This step brings this chapter neatly to a close as it is
exactly what we will cover in detail in the next chapter.

14

Creating A Pay Structure

So far in Part Three, you have learned how to:

- Develop reward principles and strategies that are aligned to your organisational values and vision

- Source external market data through the salary surveys you participate in for your comparable group of organisations and relevant locations

- Evaluate all your roles to understand their skills and responsibilities when completing your submission to participate in the pay and reward surveys

- Benchmark your roles against the salary survey data to understand how you pay compared to the external market

- Get clarity over your preferred market position (eg market median) for your pay structure

- Develop your own unique career framework with descriptions articulating what it means to be at different levels or bands within this framework

- Place all your roles (not people) on the relevant band or level within your career framework

Your next step is to analyse the data to put together a pay structure using the information you have.

Using data to create a pay structure

We can break this process down into five easy-to-follow steps.

Step 1: Understand which roles exist in your organisation

Review your data submission for the salary surveys you participated in. Which roles exist in your organisation? You can review the spreadsheet and look at the functional areas you've matched your roles to. This is the data you want to use in calculating your pay structure.

For example, let's assume you only have finance and HR roles in your organisation. To calculate a pay structure that is relevant, use finance and HR data. You don't want to use external market data for all types of roles, including sales, customer support and marketing where this data may be considerably different. This will skew your sample and you may end up with pay ranges that don't necessarily reflect the external market for the roles in your organisation.

Step 2: Carry out the data analysis

Once you have the list of functional areas that exist in your organisation, you need to gather external market data from your chosen salary survey(s) for the relevant locations. Even if your market positioning is the median, it is wise to analyse the different data points from the external market (eg 25th and 75th percentile) to get a sense of the spread of salaries.

External market data ranges tend to be closer together for junior roles, but as you get to more senior jobs, the spread of salaries from LQ to UQ, for example, gets larger. You can reflect this in your pay structure as well.

Carry out detailed data analysis for the roles in your organisation. Based on your organisation's career framework, you can then develop draft pay ranges for each career band.

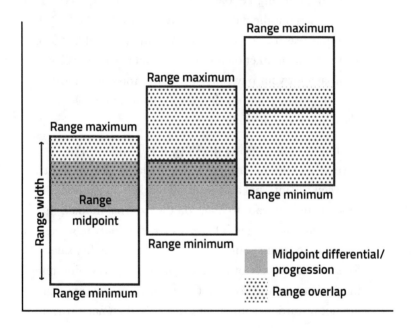

Step 3: Decide on the width of your pay ranges

Let's assume your market position is the median. If that is the midpoint of your pay range, then how wide should you make your pay ranges? For example, could they be 20% above and below the median, or 50% above and below the median? How do you decide?

There are three things to consider when making this decision:

1. Does your career framework have broad bands or narrow levels/grades? If you have a hierarchical structure with twenty grades, then it is unlikely that a wide pay range would work for your organisation, but if you have a flat structure with a handful of bands, then a wider pay range is more suited to you.

2. What does the market data tell you for your roles? When you carried out the data analysis and looked at the UQ, for example, was it 20% above the median or more like 50%? Examine the market data to understand what a sensible approach for your pay range could be. You may choose a hybrid approach with wider pay for your senior roles to allow you more flexibility.

3. A fundamental question to ask yourself when you're developing your pay ranges is what balance do you want between the internal and external market? In general, the more focus you want to place on the external market, the wider your pay ranges. This gives you flexibility to make pay increases to retain your people by offering a higher salary for some key people or roles. If your priority is maintaining internal equity and you want to ensure that your managers are not rewarding some people unfairly, then narrow ranges are more suitable for you.

Step 4: Review pay ranges against your employees and carry out an impact analysis

Having been through Steps 1–3, you may have draft pay ranges by now. You can also develop two to three options with different mid-points or pay range widths. Now you need to look at all your employees that you placed within your career framework and examine their position in your newly designed pay ranges.

If you have 100 employees, how many of them sit within the pay range for their relevant career band? How many people sit below or above the pay range? You can look at this summary for each of the different pay range options you have developed.

If you are using pay ranges and plan to publish them at some stage, which I hope you will, then you need to make sure that all employees are at least at the bottom of your pay range. If there are employees who sit below the bottom, what would be the cost of increasing salaries to bring them in line with your pay ranges? This is the impact analysis that you need to carry out for all your options.

You may want to look at different pay range widths again at this stage. The wider your pay range, the lower the cost of implementation because fewer people will sit below the bottom of your range, but this means the top of your ranges are higher and can increase your long-term costs with higher potential salaries.

Step 5: Develop your pay policy

By following Steps 1–4, you'll have your pay ranges, but how will you manage people who sit below the pay range and those who are above it? This is where you need to develop a pay policy which outlines your process and guidance on how you will manage pay issues consistently across the organisation.

Being consistent doesn't mean you can't have exceptions. Sometimes, organisations make a pay structure unnecessarily complicated to manage a few complex roles. It is better to keep things simple and consistent, but manage the small proportion of roles that are different as exceptions. You need to be clear about those exceptions and have them written down so they're documented.

Your pay policy provides clarity to issues such as what you will do with employees when they are promoted to a new band. Will their salary be increased immediately to at least the bottom of the range? Is there a minimum pay increase? Is there any guidance? This one seems straightforward, but sometimes managers are reluctant to raise a person's salary if it means a substantial (eg 40%) pay increase. The size of the increase is irrelevant if someone is currently underpaid and you make a commitment to fair and equal pay.

Other questions your pay policy should answer include:

- How will you manage people who are above the top of the pay range?

- What is your policy on promotion of employees within the same band?

- How often will you review your pay ranges against the external market? Will it be annually, for example?

- How will people progress through the pay ranges over time?

- Will the salary of employees be reviewed once a year and, if so, at what time?

- What is your policy on out-of-cycle pay increases?

Establishing pay progression in your organisation

Your career framework and pay structure help you decide how you evaluate roles within your organisation and give you guidance for managing pay, but once pay is set, you also need a framework for managing pay progression. You will have looked at this earlier as part of your reward strategy to determine *why* pay should progress in your organisation, but now you need a process to determine *how* pay will progress.

Let's assume you have a band/level with a pay range from £30,000 to £40,000. You've recruited someone at this band on a salary of £30,000. How will they progress through this pay range?

If you're going to continue to be fair and transparent, then you will need to have clear definitions and expectations. The first step is to evaluate the role by placing it on a particular band/level and the next step is evaluating the individual. To do this, you need to clearly define what you expect from employees at the entry level of the pay range (£30,000), those at the mid-point (£35,000) and those at the top of the pay range (£40,000).

This is going to be different for each organisation. To do this, you will need to speak to the leaders in your organisation who make pay decisions. This may seem like a daunting task, but use this question and it will make your job much easier.

Ask your managers to think about people within their team with similar jobs. One person is at the bottom of the range at £30,000 and the other person is at the top end of the pay range at £40,000. What is the difference between the two people in terms of their contribution that justifies this difference in salary?

Use the feedback you get to put together your definitions, which can then be communicated to employees so they understand how their pay will progress and why pay differences exist. Once you have your definitions, put them into a pay progression policy that you communicate clearly to your employees.

Creating your pay transparency project plan

Everything we've covered in Part Three is designed to give you clarity over *why* you manage pay the way you do through your reward principles and strategy, and *how* you do this through your policies and processes. How long creating a pay transparency project plan will take depends on the size and complexity of the organisation. This is not a desk exercise and you will need to find time in the diary with your leadership team to run workshops, then again to review options and approve the final output.

The table shows a summary of how long it typically takes my team at 3R Strategy to carry out each of these project steps, but just use this as a guide. We have been through this process many times, so if you're planning to do this internally, factor enough time into your project plan to build engagement with your leaders and communicate clearly to your employees.

Some of the activities can be carried out in parallel. The pay benchmarking process can begin as soon as you have run the reward principles workshop and established your comparator group and pay principles. Similarly, the career framework can begin as soon as all your roles have been evaluated, but you will need to agree on your final career framework before you can begin the analysis for your pay structure. The pay progression policy is the final step once all the other policies and processes are in place.

Reward principles and strategy	Pay benchmarking	Career framework	Pay structure	Pay progression framework
Workshop: ninety minutes Output: three to four weeks following the workshop to produce the output	Research salary surveys and agree participation: one week Evaluate all roles and submit your data: two to four weeks (depending on the number of roles) Calibration workshop to confirm levels: sixty to ninety minutes Final benchmarking report: two weeks following calibration	Building career framework options: two weeks Workshop to review options: one hour Build definitions and framework: four to eight weeks depending on the detail	Building pay structure options and impact analysis: two to three weeks Workshop to review options: one hour Full analysis of pay structure and final costing: two weeks Workshop to review and agree policy: sixty minutes Write pay policy: one week	Workshop with managers: ninety minutes (preferably three to four workshops) Pay progression policy and framework: three weeks following the last workshop

As you work through this process, you can go back to take the 3R Strategy scorecard at yourscore.3r-strategy.com to re-evaluate your score and see how it is improving. While this book has focused on helping you introduce pay transparency in your organisation, there are many ongoing activities that you need to manage such as reporting on your GPG in the UK if you have over 250 employees, carrying out an equal pay audit or managing your pay review process. You can find whitepapers and guidance on all these topics by going to 3r-strategy.com/resources.

Conclusion – We Did It!

'Well done, guys, one hour gone. Another six to go,' shouts our guide.

Has it only been an hour? I look up. We've been walking at crawling pace, heads down in pitch blackness and temperatures of -30 degrees Celsius. I wonder if I'm going to manage the rest of the six hours. I can hardly feel my hands and feet, but I keep going.

After what feels like days, our guide shouts, 'Great work, everyone. Two hours gone. Another five to go.'

I want to shout back, 'This isn't helping,' but I don't have the energy. Instead, I keep going.

As the hours pass, a mixture of altitude sickness and exhaustion causes a number of people to turn back. Oxygen levels are low. Rising to a high altitude, usually above 8,000 feet, without acclimatising can cause fluid to build up in the lungs and brain. If you get altitude sickness, there is only one solution: descend.

So far, I have made a real effort not to drink much water. There is no way I am going to risk having to use the toilet in this extreme weather. Almost halfway into our ascent, I am getting very thirsty and decide I can't put it off any longer. I reach for my water bottle, open the cap to take a sip. Nothing. My water has frozen.

Luckily, there is one person in our group who has a thermal water bottle and his water hasn't frozen. I have never shared food or drink with anyone, but these are desperate times and there is no room for irrational idiosyncrasies. We all take one sip from the bottle to keep us going.

At 6.30am, I finally reach the top of Mount Kilimanjaro at a height of over 19,000 feet. I am exhausted and can barely stand. Just then, the person from my group whose water we all shared approaches me. I don't know him that well, but he gives me a big hug and I realise he is crying.

'We did it,' he says.

Who knew climbing a mountain could be so emotional? Everyone around me has tears in their eyes, but this isn't just about climbing a mountain. They are tears of relief, exhaustion and a sense of achievement.

The freezing wind has numbed my senses along with my feet, but I now notice that the sky is starting to brighten. I look behind me and see the sun rising above an endless ocean of clouds. On either side of us, we can see glaciers in their entirety, lit up by the sun. It is unlike anything I have ever seen. Just breathtaking, and not because of the lack of oxygen.

Throughout the ascent on the final day, I was tempted to turn back, but I kept going. We all kept each other going. Although in my exhaustion, I was somewhat frustrated at our guides, later I was only grateful. We would never have made it without them; we would have been like Alice in Wonderland, not knowing which way to go.

This was by far the hardest thing I had ever done. Not just because of the physical challenge, but this was my attempt to conquer my fear of heights. Getting to the summit gave me a real sense of achievement and fulfilment – from not being able to go up in a glass lift to seeing the sun rise over Africa.

Be the shepherd

All these years later, I am in search of another seemingly impossible challenge. This time, it's in the workplace, we in HR are the guides and it's our job to make sure everyone else gets to the summit. Just like climbing Kilimanjaro, it's not going to be easy, but we can't turn back. We have to keep each other going.

When faced with a difficult task that requires me to try hard, I'm always reminded of one of my favourite films, *Pulp Fiction*.[50] Samuel L Jackson plays a gangster, Jules Winnfield, and reads out a passage from the Bible (Ezekiel 25:17, although it's not the real text) to all his victims before he shoots them.

In a nutshell, the passage tells that the path of the righteous is plagued by evil and that those who shepherd the weak are blessed. The last time Jules Winnfield reads out this passage is during a robbery in the café where he's having breakfast with Vincent Vega, played by John Travolta, but this time he decides not to shoot the robber. He believes he has just witnessed a miracle. Someone shot at him several times from point-blank range and missed every time. Now for the first time, he is re-evaluating his life and actually thinking about what this passage means.

Jules considers who in this situation is righteous, evil and the shepherd. He wonders aloud whether the robber, Pumpkin, could be the evil man, Jules himself the righteous man and his gun the shepherd – or even whether Pumpkin could be righteous, Jules the shepherd and it's the world that is evil.

Ultimately, Jules knows that he represents evil and Pumpkin 'the weak', but says he's 'tryin' real hard to be the shepherd'.

---

50   Tarantino, Q, *Pulp Fiction* (Miramax Films, 1994)

I hope this book has provided you with a good understanding of how to create a more transparent approach to pay in your organisation. An approach that is fair and has the incredible potential to transform your organisation's culture, building trust with your colleagues and boosting productivity.

The lesson from *Pulp Fiction* is the same as the lesson Coach Taylor gives in *Friday Night Lights*. You don't have to be the best or be able to do everything, but you've got to try and that's what character is. It's in the trying.

Unlike Jules Winnfield, we as HR team members don't need to witness a miracle to re-evaluate our profession. We already know why our profession is so important. In this roadmap to pay transparency, we have a blueprint of exactly what we need to do to give our people meaning in their work.

It often requires a change in mindset in our organisations, particularly from the leaders we work with. A culture built on trust where we believe that people are fundamentally good. Of course, there will be people along the journey who will betray our trust, but the benefit of doing things the right way for the vast majority of our people far outweighs the impact of a few bad apples.

If we believe that people are fundamentally good, then maybe the passage read out by Jules Winnfield tells us that the employee is the righteous person and we as HR have to be the shepherds. Who knows? Maybe one day we'll be at the summit of the mountain, giving our HR colleagues a big hug and saying, 'We did it'.

Acknowledgements

Writing a book was never on my bucket list. Neither was starting my own business, but having a sense of purpose can make us all do things we never expected!

Quitting a good corporate job to venture out into the unknown world of setting up a business on my own was a daunting task, but I've always had the support of my parents and family.

I didn't really know where to start and this book wouldn't have been possible without the coaching, guidance and support from many people.

I spent years volunteering and managing projects with the charities The City Circle and Remembering Srebrenica. I am gaining all my pay and reward knowledge from my professional career, but I probably would never have had the confidence or skills to set up my own business if it wasn't for everything I learned from these projects and the other volunteers I worked with.

I'd like to thank a few authors who inspired me through their books, influencing my career as well as ideas. These include Simon Sinek, Brene Brown, Matthew Syed, Laszlo Bock, Daniel Priestley and, in particular, Susan Cain. The book *Quiet* by Susan Cain[51] was partly responsible for me leaving my corporate career, where I didn't feel a sense of belonging, to set up my own business.

---

51   Cain, S, *Quiet: The power of introverts in a world that can't stop talking* (Penguin, 2013)

When I first began writing the book, I really needed guidance and was lucky enough to get some coaching from Sheryl Green.

I'd like to thank the team at 3R Strategy. Because of this team, I now never have a case of the Mondays. In fact, I look forward to our weekly team meeting on Mondays.

I'm not sure how I would have got this book completed without the support of Jenna Thompson from the 3R Strategy team, with her attention to detail, insight and creative input. I wanted to share my vision and guidance through the book, but also make it fun and memorable. Jenna and I spent many hours brainstorming ideas and were fortunate to have the creative support of AnneMarie Walsh who drew the amazing illustrations.

Finally, I'd like to thank the entire team at Rethink Press, who have been supportive and a pleasure to work with throughout the process.

The Author

Rameez is the founder and managing director at 3R Strategy, an independent reward consultancy dedicated to helping organisations build a culture of trust through pay transparency.

Rameez graduated in economics from University College London and began his career in consultancy, initially working in global mobility and then as a reward consultant at Willis Towers Watson. He worked in several in-house reward roles before quitting the corporate world to set up 3R Strategy to support organisations on their journey towards pay transparency.

With over twenty years in pay and reward, he consults extensively on these topics, speaking regularly in HR forums and podcasts.

You can connect with Rameez or find out more about 3R Strategy and join the mailing list.

🌐 3r-strategy.com

in linkedin.com/in/rameezkaleem

CPSIA information can be obtained
at www.ICGtesting.com
Printed in the USA
LVHW051942220623
750554LV00001B/129